TIM LOWRY

STORYTELLER

SOUTHERN FRIED CIRCUS

ISBN: 979-8-9893061-2-1

Produced by Publish Pros | publishpros.com

To my mom

TABLE OF CONTENTS

INTRODUCTION

Seated in 21C, I began composing my speech. The flight attendant was working her way down the aisle, dispensing soft drinks and pretzels and making small talk with each passenger. She was just doing her job, but I sort of dreaded our conversation. I hate small talk. As a professional storyteller, I value deep and meaningful conversation, but common courtesy often requires bland chit chat. Consequently, I stress more over the short and simple speech than the long, drawn-out yarn. I listened to her brief exchange with the passenger in front of me.

"Would you like a soft drink?"

"Yes, Diet Coke please."

"Pretzels?"

"No, thank you."

"Are you traveling for business or pleasure?"

"Business meeting, I'm in marketing."

"I hope your meeting goes well. Here's your Diet Coke."

"Thank you."

"My pleasure."

Except for various soft drink preferences, this conversation was pretty much like every one that had come before it. Then it was my turn.

"Would you like a soft drink?"

I panicked. I'm simply not good at this kind of thing. "I would like a Coke, but where I come from most people say 'Co-cola.' It's too bad this is a peanut-free flight, because there's nothing better than dumping a pack of goobers down the neck of an icy cold bottle and sipping the salty fizz that comes squirting out the top."

The flight attendant laughed. "My daddy used to do that. Are you traveling for business or pleasure?"

I answered truthfully. "My business is my pleasure. I am a professional storyteller."

"Professional storyteller? What's that like?"

"Well, I travel all over the country sleeping in hotels, eating at twenty-four-hour diners, and performing in theaters, churches, libraries, schools, and other venues. This time I'm headed to the Timpanogos Storytelling Festival near Salt Lake City, where I shall dress in my signature seersucker suit to stand on a stage under a big white tent with seating for over a thousand people to talk about the time I accidentally set a goat on fire, learned to ride a unicycle, and trained the world's only kissing duck."

She laughed even more and said, "Here's that Co-cola, you Southern Fried Circus." I apologized for taking up so much time, but she replied, "Not at all. You should write a book."

So, I did.

MY CIRCUS MOM

"Ladies and gentlemen! Children of all ages! Kids from one to one-hundred-and-one! Irvin Feld and Kenneth Feld are proud to present, here in the beautiful Civic Coliseum of Knoxville, Tennessee, the one-hundred-and-fifth edition of the Ringling Brothers and Barnum and Bailey Circus!"

I was not like other children.

When I was growing up, people would always ask, "Are you going to be a preacher like your daddy?"

I always hated that. I loved my daddy, and I loved the Lord, but I did not want to be a preacher. Nope. It was not the still, small voice of the Holy Spirit that called to me from way down deep in the recesses of my heart. Quite the opposite. It was the megaphoned voice of a circus ringmaster, dressed in a red tailcoat and shiny black top hat, illuminated by a bright spotlight, and standing in the center ring before 30,000 fans.

"In ring one, a cavalcade of characters, with crazy cars, kooky contraptions, and cataclysmic comedy—the Clown Alley!

"Over ring two, high above the arena floor, the first aerialist to complete the quadruple somersault with astounding acrobatic acumen and amazing agility—Miguel Vazquez!

"And in ring three, a procession of prodigious pachyderms on pompous parade—the Ringling Brothers elephants!"

Seeing the circus at six years of age, I immediately wanted to be in show business. I couldn't get enough of that atmosphere—the costumes, the swirling lights, the roar of the crowd, the unique aroma of buttered popcorn mixed with the smell of elephant dung. I loved it!

Years later, I asked my mom when she first realized I would grow up to be a performer. She didn't even stop to think before answering, "When you saw the circus for the first time, I saw it on your face. I didn't know what path would get you there, but I knew you were going to be a showman."

You may think a mother couldn't possibly be certain of such a thing from the expression on her boy's face. However, you don't know my mother. She has been legally blind from birth. (As a kid, I always thought that was such a strange term. Legally blind. As if it was against the law to see well.) Because of her visual impairment, she really couldn't see any of the show on the arena floor. Instead, she spent the whole time watching me as I watched "The Greatest Show on Earth."

I came home from the circus with the full-color souvenir program. And for weeks, months, and even years, I pored over every page of it, trying to figure out what kind of circus act I wanted to perfect. There was a feature article about Michu, the smallest man in the world. He was only thirty-three inches tall. I concluded that getting into the circus would be fairly easy. All I had to do was never grow taller than three inches short of a yard stick. However, my hope of out-smalling the smallest man in the world was dashed when my mom showed me pencil marks on the kitchen door frame where she tracked my growth. I was already a head and a half taller than Michu. His job was secure.

I read about master clowns like Frosty Little, Lou Jacobs, and Barry Lubin. Other boys quoted statistics about baseball players, I knew circus clowns. Frosty was a classic whiteface, but Lou was auguste. The auguste clown popularized the red, rubber nose. Barry was a character clown. He dressed as a groovy granny and rode a skateboard. Clowns working for Ringling Brothers had to have perfect pantomime skills. Since they performed in 30,000-seat arenas, their acts had to be all physical comedy. No talking. My mother would quickly tell you nobody had to teach me how to talk. There was no way I could be a silent showman.

Finally, I discovered the world-renowned animal trainer Gunther Gebel-Williams. Now there was a job for me! Gunther had twenty-one elephants, thirty-eight horses, twenty-two tigers, four zebras, three camels, and a couple llamas. I only had three goats—a milk goat and two kids—but it was a start. There is nothing more agile than a young goat. I taught my goats how to walk on their hind legs, trip-trap over a little bridge, and balance on a teeter board. I even taught the mother goat to pray. That was my dad's idea, him being a preacher and all. On the command "time to say your prayers," the nanny goat would piously kneel with her head to the ground. Friends and neighbors thought the act was pretty good, but "pretty good" would never get me into the circus as a featured performer. My act had to be more showy, more colorful. It needed razzle dazzle.

One afternoon, while I was working with my goats, I was struck by a sudden thought: "I bet they've never had a super flying goat before!" I ran into the house and took a big, square scarf from my mom's top dresser drawer. Bright pink and very showy, the silk chiffon looked beautiful when I tied it around my goat's neck. It ran the entire length of her back and hung down on both sides, just like the bejeweled drapes worn by elephants and horses in the circus parades.

I spent all afternoon teaching my goat to fly one small step at a time. First, I laid a broomstick on the ground. With the goat on a leash, I walked her across the broomstick several times, giving her a small food treat each time she stepped over. Soon enough, she voluntarily stepped over the broomstick with ease. Then I laid the broomstick across the top of a couple boxes and coaxed the goat to step over the hurdle. She didn't even have to jump. Next, I stacked a couple more boxes on top of the first two and lay the broomstick across. It took a little practice, but with plenty of coaxing and a little bribery in the form of a handful of goat chow, I got her to jump up and over. We practiced again and again until my goat could easily soar through the air with that pink cape billowing in the wind. I had taken my animal act from "pretty good" to "pretty great." But my ambition was growing. I wanted to take it from great to gargantuan.

Gargantua the Great was the largest and fiercest gorilla ever brought before the eyes of civilized man when he toured with the Ringling Brothers and Barnum and Bailey Circus for nearly two decades during the first half of the twentieth century. Ever since then, anything big, really big, has been known as "gargantuan." (No extra charge for that little bit of circus trivia.)

Any circus star can tell you the essential element for a gargantuan performance—fire! All the necessary supplies were conveniently located on my dad's BBQ grill: some old rags to wrap around the broomstick, a bottle of lighter fluid to soak the rags, and a big box of long-stemmed, wooden matches. I also made sure my pockets were full of goat chow.

At a safe distance, I struck a match and lit the rags wrapped around the broomstick. My goat jumped back. Taking up the leash and digging into my pocket for a little goat chow, I trotted her around in a big circle before we made a turn toward the flames. She started to balk, but then she just went for it, soaring high into the air with a twisting motion that made the winged flight of the legendary Pegasus look like a cheap wind-up toy! My super flying goat cleared the bar with sixteen inches to spare ... but the tail end of her billowing cape caught fire.

Instantly I had two showbiz superlatives to my credit. The world's only super flying goat was also the fastest running goat in circus history! Tearing the leash out of my hand, she went streaking over the yard like a comet from outer space, flying up and over the fence, across the field, and halfway to the milk shed before I could catch up to her. The silk had burned up in a literal flash, without leaving so much as a scrap. Miraculously the goat was unharmed, but she would never come near me after that.

There was no hiding what I had done from my mother. Especially since I needed her help to catch the goat, extinguish the flaming broomstick, and clean up the mess. Not to mention her missing pink, silk chiffon scarf.

She calmly listened to the whole story. "Ducks. You may work with ducks."

I didn't have to ask why, because the reason was obvious: water.

I got to work immediately, filling a kiddie pool with the garden hose. Then I went into the house and took a sleeve of saltine crackers from the kitchen cabinet. With crackers in hand, I followed the winding path from our backyard, across the railroad tracks, and down to the riverbank where we kept a flock of six ducks. I opened the sleeve of saltines, crumbled a few crackers, and tossed them onto the ground. The ducks swam right over to gobble up the treat. I kept dropping cracker crumbs as I walked back up the path to the house. In no time, the ducks followed the cracker crumb trail across the tracks, up the hill, and into the backyard, where they immediately jumped into the kiddie pool.

That was the easy part; as they say, "Ducks to water." The real trick turned out to be teaching them to do something fantastic. Besides swimming, ducks are only good at two things: eating and pooping. This was going to be a challenge. I failed at teaching them to swim through a hoop. I was equally unsuccessful in getting my ducks in a row. Excuse the pun, but they simply would not line up in a formation. Finally, I consulted my full-color circus program for some inspiration and discovered a picture of my hero Gunther Gebel-Williams standing inside a tiger cage with a small piece of meat clenched between his teeth. A big Bengal stood up on his hind legs with his paws on Gunther's shoulders. The tiger was about to pluck the meat from the animal trainer's teeth, making it look like he was giving Gunther a big, wet kiss. A loving tiger was one thing, an amorous duck would be quite another.

When my goat wore a cape, things ended in near disaster. So this time I wore the costume. Donning the long black cape from an old Halloween costume, I billed myself "Darth Vader and His Kissing Quacker!" I was certain Ringling Brothers had never seen anything like it before. One duck, named Caboose, was always last when the flock came waddling into the backyard. Caboose was the star of my show. As I swooped down toward the kiddie pool, spreading the cape behind me with a dramatic flair, she would swim right over and stretch out her neck to snatch a saltine cracker held between my teeth. Then she would imitate me in my big cape as she backed away, flapping her wings and quacking loudly. (To be honest, I'm not certain she was imitating me. She may have been scared to death whenever Darth Vader hovered menacingly over her kiddie pool with a saltine cracker clenched between his teeth. Nonetheless, the effect was very dramatic and served my purpose well.)

I was on my way to circus stardom with a kissing duck named Caboose. Unfortunately, the circus life is fraught with danger and peril. Caboose's promising career was cut short when disaster struck one fateful Saturday afternoon.

I was leading the ducks up the path from the riverbank for a practice session. Just as we started over the railroad tracks, I heard a train engine blow its horn. I hurried across and frantically started crushing saltine crackers and scattering the crumbs. The ducks waddled across the tracks one by one, but Caboose, my star kisser, was in the back of the line. There was still time, but she seemed oblivious to the approaching danger. When the engine blared the horn again, instead of rushing out of harm's way she assumed her defensive position by turning to face the locomotive with her wings spread out wide, flapping and quacking for all she was worth. I was horrified! Unable to do anything else, I threw down the remaining saltine crackers, covered my face with my hands, and immediately began composing a eulogy to rival that of Jumbo's. (Jumbo was the largest elephant ever kept in captivity. Weighing 13,558 pounds, he was P.T. Barnum's greatest attraction. Fatally wounded in a railway accident in Ontario, Canada on September 15, 1885, his death was met with worldwide grief and sorrow.)

I know not how, because my eyes were closed, but my duck managed to defy death. I would guess at the last available second, she had backed off the railroad tracks, still flapping her wings and quacking hysterically. Since her bill was the last part of her body to clear the rail, the train wheels had clipped it right off. It was a clean cut, not unlike clipping your fingernail, with no blood or gore. Fortunately, she had rolled her tongue into the back of her mouth. That vital organ had not received even the slightest injury, but my duck could no longer grab a cracker from my teeth. She couldn't even quack; she just waddled around with her tongue hanging out, flapped her wings, and went "Blehhh!" My world-famous feature act, The Kissing Quacker, had been reduced to a carnival freak show!

This near tragedy helped me realize I could not ride on the tail feathers of a duck into the circus, but after reading about The King Charles Troupe, a unicycle seemed to be the perfect vehicle. The King Charles Troupe originated in New York City as a youth program for teens. Ringling

Brothers producers discovered them entertaining crowds on the street outside Madison Square Garden. Not unlike the world-famous Harlem Globetrotters, these fellows also played basketball, but performed their hijinks while riding unicycles.

Growing up in Kentucky, I was very familiar with the sport of basketball. It was almost like a religion. What was unfamiliar was the unicycle. When I was about twelve years old, I asked my parents if I could have one for Christmas. They happily obliged and tossed in a rainbow-colored wig and a red, rubber nose as stocking stuffers. I found a red-and-white striped zip-up union suit in a costume bin at the local thrift store to complete my ensemble. But a fabulous costume alone does not make an accomplished unicyclist. Learning to ride that thing proved more than a little challenging, especially living out in the country where there were no sidewalks or parking lots to practice. The only smooth, paved surface anywhere around was the quarter mile stretch of two-lane road that ran in front of our house. Unlike a suburban cul-de-sac where kids can safely ride bikes and roller skates, this well-traveled piece of highway had dead-man curves on either end. However, my mom came up with a solution.

Several evenings each week, after supper was done, she would make two steaming hot cups of coffee. Taking one cup Mom would walk down the road to the nearest curve and my dad would take the other cup and walk in the opposite direction. I would practice unicycle tricks and bounce a basketball while my parents stood in the curves, sipping coffee and flagging traffic. The first time we tried this arrangement, I worried that with her poor vision, my mom wouldn't see me and might accidentally let a car through to run me over. As I expressed this concern standing before her in my striped union suit, rainbow wig, and red, rubber nose, she just smiled and said, "Don't worry, if I can't see you, the driver certainly will."

It took about two years to master the unicycle. By that time, I had started high school where I could try out for a basketball team. That was my undoing, and tragically, the end of my circus career. I was the worst basketball player in the history of the sport. At first, because of my height, the coach thought I had potential for the position of center, but when he observed my ball-handling ability (or should I say inability), he said, "You keep working with that one-wheel bicycle, son. You ain't never going to get a basketball scholarship, but there's always clown college."

I haven't ridden a unicycle since. They say once you learn to ride a bicycle you never forget. I don't know if it's the same for a unicycle, but I'm sure the clown and his mother at mile marker seven on Highway 119 provided a very memorable experience for many a motorist as the world's only drive-through circus.

I left basketball tryouts to audition for drama club. It was there that I discovered a group of teenagers just as weird as me. My junior year I joined a summer theatre troupe, landing a role in a Broadway-style musical. We were booked for a three-month East Coast tour with seven shows a week. I considered it the opportunity of a lifetime, but since I was a student and not a professional actor, the position was unpaid. In fact, I had to pay dues for a slot in the show, which would require a considerable amount of fundraising.

My mom worked at a little country store that sold milk, bread, and other convenience items. There was also a lunch counter serving fresh sandwiches and hot dogs, and a couple gas pumps out front. Local workmen would pull up to the gas pumps for a fill-up and come inside to buy a sandwich or hot dog for lunch. A number of these men were on the lazy side. Having purchased a couple hot dogs, a bag of chips, and an RC Cola, they would sit down on a bench, expecting my mom to leave the lunch counter and pump the gasoline into their trucks while they ate their food.

Noticing their work trucks were always covered in grime and dirt, my mom came up with the perfect fundraising plan. When these men were ready to check out, she would say, "Your truck is filthy. My son has a truck washing business. Why don't you sit back down and have a Little Debbie snack cake for dessert while my son washes your truck? It will take just a few minutes and cost you only ten dollars."

And just like that I was making money for my trip. I washed trucks throughout the spring, but as the time approached for my summer theatre tour, I was still short about a hundred bucks.

Once again, my mom had it all figured out: "We'll sell dogs!"

Our German shepherd had given birth to a beautiful litter of ten puppies. Mom put up a sign at the store advertising "Puppies for sale! Ten dollars each!" When folks expressed interest, Mom would put their name on a list. After the puppies were weaned, she planned to call and let them know their dog was ready. In no time at all, we had a list of eight interested people, which left only two puppies unspoken for.

One afternoon, a fellow came into the store saying he might want to put his name down for the remaining two pups, but he needed to go home and check with his wife. In the meantime, another fellow came into the store. He looked very much like the first one, and my mother has very poor vision.

"Excuse me, do you still have some dogs?"

My mom answered enthusiastically. "I got two left and they both have your name on them."

The man looked a little puzzled. "Well, I was thinking only one, but if you already got my name on them, give me the two."

My mom picked up a pad of paper and a pen. "What's your phone number?" When the man asked why she needed his phone number, Mom explained, "So I can call you when they're ready."

"Well, how long is this going to take?" asked the man.

"At least six weeks," she replied. "They're not even weaned yet. Oh, and what sex do you want? Two males, two females, or one of each?"

Finally, the man said in a rather exasperated tone, "Lady, I'm trying to order two HOT DOGS!"

My mother, mortified, tried to explain the confusion. Before she had finished telling the whole crazy story the customer was laughing out loud.

"So you're raising money for your son's theatre trip by selling German shepherd puppies?"

My mother answered in the affirmative as she handed him his two hot dogs.

"Well I'm allergic, but here ya go. Your son can keep the change." Then he handed my mom a hundred-dollar bill.

When my summer theatre group toured New York City all the other kids bought "I Love New York" t-shirts and posters from their favorite Broadway shows, but I went looking for a different sort of souvenir. I found a street vendor selling kitschy knick-knacks and purchased a little porcelain German shepherd dog with a rhinestone collar to take home to my mom.

After high school my family moved to Greenville, South Carolina, where I entered college as a theatre major to study Shakespeare. I auditioned for a part in the fall production of *Julius Caesar*. Taking my circus experience and high school theatre classes into account, the director cast me in the role of Octavius, which, if I may brag a little bit, ain't too shabby for a freshman.

I lived at home and commuted to class each day. My mom was teaching at a local kindergarten. Since she couldn't see well enough to drive, I would give her a ride to work every morning before driving to my classes, and my dad would pick her up in the afternoons. So five days a week I would have a nice car chat with my mom. As rehearsals got rolling for *Julius Caesar*, I needed to memorize my lines.

One morning I tossed a copy of the script into my mom's lap and said, "While I'm driving, read the cues from act five aloud and I'll quote lines. You follow along and correct me if I miss anything."

My mom took one look at the small print and said, "I can't see that. You're on your own." She tossed the script into the backseat of the car. When I started to fuss and fret about not being ready for that evening's rehearsal she said, "Well, there's only one thing to do. How does the scene start?"

"What do you mean?"

"The scene you're rehearsing, what's your first line?"

"Well, I enter and say, 'Now, Antony, our hopes are answered. You said the enemy would not come down, but keep to the hills and upper regions. It proves not so, their battles are at hand.'"

I paused and my mom asked, "Is that it?"

"Yeah, that's what I say."

"So, who speaks next?"

"Well, Mark Antony says, 'Tut, they come down with fearful bravery, thinking by this face to fasten in our thoughts that they have courage, but 'tis not so.'"

When I finished quoting Mark Antony's line I didn't immediately say anything else. My mom prodded me. "Is that the end of the scene? Doesn't seem like there's very much to it. I don't know what you were so worried about."

I had unknowingly taken the bait. "No, there's plenty more," I explained. "A messenger comes running in and says, 'Prepare you generals! The enemy comes in a gallant show. Their bloody sign of battle is hung out and something to be done immediately!'"

My mom then slyly asked, "How does your character respond to such news?"

I launched into my favorite speech. "Come, come, the cause! Look, I draw a sword against conspirators! When think you that the sword goes up again? Never, 'til Caesar's three and thirty wounds be well avenged; or 'til another Caesar have added slaughter to the sword of traitors!"

Responding to my mother's prompting, I continued spouting lines. Just before dropping her off at her kindergarten, I realized that I had quoted the majority of act five from Shakespeare's *Julius Caesar*. As she got out the car my mom quipped, "Don't mistake this for a standing ovation. I'm just going into work. Nonetheless, I thought you were terrific. Have a good play practice."

Rehearsal days were very, very long. I would drop my mom at her job around seven thirty, then drive to college for a full day of classes. As a work-study student, I went to a local elementary school every afternoon at four and cleaned bathrooms for two hours. At six, I would clock out and drive back to campus to attend a three-hour rehearsal, after which I would return to the elementary school to complete two hours of vacuuming. Finally arriving at home just before eleven thirty, I would fall into bed and get up the next morning at six to do it all over again.

The day my mom tricked me into quoting act five from *Julius Caesar*, I had completed everything on my marathon schedule except clocking back into the elementary school to do the vacuuming. I was playing a general from ancient times in a Shakespearean tragedy, but by that point in the day I was more exhausted than a Roman galley slave. When I walked up to the door of the school office and thrust my key into the lock, I noticed someone had left a sticky note. I pulled the note off the door and recognized my mother's handwriting.

"Come, come, the cause! Look, I have drawn thy vacuum cleaner over three and thirty classrooms. When think you that it shall be put up again? Not until my son has finished his run as Octavius in the fall production of *Julius Caesar*! Comest thou home. Thy supper is in the refrigerator."

For all the remaining rehearsal days, my mom had my dad drive her over to the elementary school where she vacuumed for me so I could keep my work-study status, star in my first Shakespearean play, and still get home at a decent hour every night.

After seeing the show in the theatre, she came backstage to congratulate me. "I couldn't really tell if that was you on the stage until you spoke. Then I recognized you by your voice, and I already knew all the lines."

✷✷✷

When I finished college, I moved to Charleston, South Carolina, where I eventually found my niche in the world of show business. Not long after I started working as a professional storyteller, the circus came to town. Circus Flora was a one-ring, European-style traveling tent show featuring the world-famous highwire daredevils, The Flying Wallendas! Well of course, on opening night I was seated in the very front row.

Just before intermission, the feature act was presented, a classic highwire routine with the typical feats of strength and balance: jumping rope, riding a bicycle, walking the wire blindfolded.

At last, the ringmaster announced the finale. "Ladies and gentlemen! Please remain in your seats, withhold your applause, and refrain from any flash photography as The Flying Wallendas perform their signature stunt—the death-defying Seven Man Pyramid!"

It was one of the greatest showbiz moments I have ever witnessed. With the rest of the audience, I sat with my mouth gaping open, stunned into silence, as the pyramid was built. First, two young men stepped out onto the wire, one in front of the other. They each wore a shoulder harness that allowed a pole to be suspended between them. After these two men walked some distance across the wire, another pair of men, also wearing harnesses and bearing a pole, stepped out behind them. These four men held steady while two more men climbed up and over their shoulders to stand balanced, one man each, on the two suspended poles. These two men also had shoulder harnesses and a suspended pole between them. Next, a young girl with a chair in her hand, climbed to the top of this pyramid. After she had carefully balanced the chair on the uppermost pole, she stood up in the chair!

The audience maintained such a silence that I could hear my own heart throbbing. Finally, when it was safe to do so, the musicians began to play, not a traditional circus fanfare, but a hymn. In that moment The Flying Wallendas had achieved what every great show strives for—strong, capable, fearless individuals working together in unity to show how vulnerable, dependent, and terrifying the human condition can be. It was truly nothing short of amazing grace.

When the band finished the hymn, I glanced down from the wire overhead to the floor below to verify what I had always heard. I saw with my own eyes that the story was true. The Flying Wallendas work without a net. However, they were not without safety measures. Mrs. Wallenda, the mother of two of those young men and the grandmother of the young girl balanced so precariously more than forty feet in the air, was down on her knees in the sawdust, fervently praying for the safety of her family as they performed for the crowd.

At last, the performers began their careful walk to the far end of the wire. When the tedious business of disassembling the pyramid was safely accomplished, Mrs. Wallenda rose from her kneeling position, and with a showbiz smile second-to-none, gestured toward the skies as the crowd burst into applause with a standing ovation lasting several minutes.

After the show, I went home to call my mom. "I went to the circus today!"

Knowing full well her response was a gross understatement, she simply replied, "Oh, I bet that brought back some memories."

She waited for me to speak again, but my mind was swirling with images of pink chiffon fluttering in the breeze, a goat soaring through the air, a white duck flapping her wings, a unicycle parked in one corner of my parents' garage, a whole parade of filthy work trucks, an audience applauding Octavius's dramatic speech from act five of *Julius Caesar* ... and the unique aroma of buttered popcorn mixed with the smell of elephant dung.

When I finally spoke, all I could say was "Thank you."

To which she replied, "You're welcome."

Ladies and gentlemen! Children of all ages! Kids from one to one-hundred-and-one! Storyteller Tim Lowry stands to remind all circus performers, high school theatre students, and Shakespearean actors that every success you will ever achieve is due in no small part to the biggest star of all...YOUR MOTHER!

GROWING UP

A TRIP TO DISNEY WORLD

As you know, I was raised a Baptist preacher's kid, which meant we went to church three times a week without fail. Sunday morning, Sunday night, and Wednesday night. Considered essential for spiritual well-being, these weekly meetings were often referred to as "the three to thrive." On Sunday mornings, I was entertained by listening to my daddy preach with lots of hellfire and brimstone. On Sunday nights, we always had extra singing. You can't help but have a good time during a singing service at a country Baptist church equipped with an old-fashioned upright piano and folks who can carry all four parts for good harmony. But on Wednesday night, there was only a simple prayer service. My dad would read some scripture and give a very short devotional, then everybody divided into prayer groups.

There was no prayer group for children, so all of us kids had to go with our mothers. The mothers would pray. And pray. And pray. Eventually we children would begin to pray that our mothers would stop praying so we could go outside and play in the graveyard. Playing hide-and-seek among the tombstones after dark somewhat made up for the tediously long prayers.

Sitting next to my mother on Wednesday nights week after week, I learned the language of prayer. I heard the ladies say things like "Seek and ye shall find." "Knock, and it shall be opened unto you." "The Lord will give you the desire of your heart." As a six-year-old Baptist, my heart only had one great desire: I wanted to go to Disney World! But I knew that when it was time to give prayer requests, you couldn't stand up in the middle of the ladies' prayer circle and say, "The desire of my heart is to go to Disney World." That's just not spiritually correct. In a Baptist ladies' prayer group, you're supposed to pray for starving children in China, the Lottie Moon missionary offering, and stuff like that. (Lottie Moon was a nineteenth-century missionary to China. Whenever Baptists take up a collection of money for foreign missions they call it the Lottie Moon Offering. I'm not sure they realize she's been dead for over a hundred years. Nobody knows where that money is going!)

I couldn't just blurt out what I really wanted, but luckily I had learned how to present my need in a more spiritually acceptable way. This prayer request technique is usually reserved for women who are suffering hot flashes because they are going through menopause, but they don't want to say as much out loud.

One Wednesday evening, I raised my hand and said, "I have an unspoken prayer request." And without asking any embarrassing questions, the ladies of the prayer circle prayed for me.

I knew God had answered my prayer when my daddy sat down at the breakfast table the very next morning and out of the blue said, "We haven't had a vacation in a couple years. Your mother and I talked it over last night. We're going to take you and your sister to Disney World!"

Yes! There was a God and He loved me!

Then the news got even better, because my dad continued, "Let's go in the fall. You'll miss a little school, but I don't think that will hurt. Besides, in October the park won't be as crowded and the weather won't be so terribly hot."

Not only was I going to Disney World, but I also got to miss school! My faith was growing exponentially.

As the time grew closer for our trip, my dad reminded my sister and me about expectations for the long car ride. He showed us in the road atlas how far it would be to drive from our home in Kentucky all the way to Orlando, Florida—nearly 800 miles!

"Now you're going to have to entertain yourselves. I don't want any whining and fussing, or yelling from the back seat 'Are we there yet?'"

He needn't have worried, because we already had a plan for the long drive. We were going to play *"Emergency!"* That was our favorite television show. It was on NBC every Thursday night. We never missed it. The show offered plenty of action and adventure with Johnny Gage and Roy DeSoto, two young firefighting paramedics from Station 51, and the intrepid medical staff at Rampart General

Hospital. Johnny and Roy would be dispatched from the fire station to assist a citizen of Los Angeles who was in grave danger. Arriving on the scene with sirens blaring, they would quickly assess the situation, then place a call on their portable phone, which was the size of a large briefcase.

"Rampart, we have a patient approximately fifty-seven years of age with heart palpitations. His skin is clammy, breathing shallow, BP is one eighty over one twenty. Over."

Then a doctor at the hospital would respond. "Copy that fifty-one. Start an IV with ringers and bring him right in. Over and out."

Those dramatic rescue scenes convinced us kids you could never die if you had an IV with ringers. Sometimes it might be touch-and-go, but even if rigor mortis was already setting in, the patient would somehow pull through.

Our family drove a Ford Pinto station wagon, which was perfect for playing *"Emergency!"* because at that time ambulances were shaped like station wagons. We would lay all the back seats down flat to make enough room to accommodate a patient laying on a gurney. Back then nobody made you wear a seatbelt. Any time we were on a long drive, my sister and I would put the seats down and climb all over that car. That changed when I was older due to the newly introduced and strictly enforced seatbelt laws. After a long drive, I would joke with my mom saying, "I'm going to call the Department of Social Services and report you for child abuse. You kept me tied to a car for six hours!"

We would get all the supplies we needed for playing *"Emergency!"* at McDonald's. In those days, McDonald's did not serve Happy Meals. All the menu items came wrapped in plain white paper. But that was perfect because it looked just like hospital stuff. After we ate our food, my sister and I would take the little white French fry bag and hang it from the coat hook above the back window. Then we'd link several soda straws to make a long tube running down from the bag with the end tucked under the patient's shirt sleeve. A hamburger paper with a little ketchup on it looked like blood. You could slap it on the patient's head and pretend they had suffered a contusion. If it was your turn to be the poor trauma victim laying in the back of the Ford Pinto station wagon with a nearly fatal head injury, you never worried because you were hooked up to a French fry soda straw IV with ringers.

About three days before our trip, the phone rang. It was probably this particular moment that made that phone, which hung on the wall in the kitchen, such a vivid image in my memory. Its harvest gold color contrasted with my mother's avocado green stove. There was a big, long cord attached to the receiver looping all the way down to the burnt orange linoleum floor. We loved that phone. Like the Ford Pinto station wagon, it was not meant to be a toy, but we would play with it anyway. When my mom talked on the phone the extra-long cord allowed her to walk around the kitchen. With the cord stretched across the room, it made a perfect jump rope. That always made my mom so mad. She would start slapping at us with the cord and hissing, "Stop it! I am on the phone!"

However, on this occasion Mom didn't walk around the kitchen. She just stood still, mostly listening to someone on the other end of the line. Finally, she hung up the receiver and turned to face us.

"Uncle Bill died."

So we had to cancel our trip to Disney World and go to a funeral in Mississippi. You know what they have in Mississippi? Nothing! We loved our Uncle Bill, but this was a major letdown for sure.

After the funeral we stayed for several days to help my newly widowed Aunt Sissy get situated. Uncle Bill and Aunt Sissy had a teenage daughter named Linda Joyce. As her little kid cousins, we thought she was cool with her bell-bottom blue jeans and dangly earrings. She even drove her own car. Well, as you can imagine, after her daddy's funeral Linda Joyce was not her usual fun and sassy self. She was grieving, which was to be expected, but it seemed strange to me and my little sister that Linda Joyce was angry. Of course anger is definitely a part of the grieving process but Linda Joyce wasn't angry at God for allowing her daddy to die. She was ticked off that her little cousins didn't get to take their trip to Disney World.

Since it was October, Halloween was approaching. Linda Joyce decided she wanted to try and make it up to us by taking us trick-or-treating. I remember her saying,

"Dang it! The least we can do is take you around to some houses and help you get a sack full of candy."

She took us to the store to buy some last-minute Halloween costumes, but all the good stuff was gone. We searched around in a bin of picked-over odds and ends and found, of all things, two pairs of Mickey Mouse ears. Linda Joyce snorted. "No trip to the Magic Kingdom but you end up with the head gear. Talk about irony!"

We didn't know what "irony" meant, but we took the Mickey Mouse ears. She also bought us flashlights with plastic skulls mounted on the end. When you flipped the switch, the eyes would light up bright red.

On Halloween night we donned our Mickey Mouse ears and grabbed those glowing skull flashlights. Linda Joyce completed our costumes by pinning black, plastic garbage bags to our shoulders to serve as makeshift capes. We took a pillowcase for collecting candy and climbed into the back seat of her Ford LTD. When we pulled away from Uncle Bill and Aunt Sissy's farmhouse, Linda Joyce stomped on the gas pedal and we went roaring down the dirt road. The first curve sent my sister and I, sitting on those plastic garbage bag capes, sliding across the back seat. Then she whipped around another curve and we slid back in the opposite direction. We thought that was fun, maybe as good as one of the rides at Disney World.

After a short, wild ride, we pulled up into the yard of another farmhouse. Linda Joyce honked the horn as we climbed out of the back of the car and ran toward the front door. One of her high school girlfriends stepped out onto the porch. Holding a big bowl of treats, she looked us up and down with our Mickey Mouse ears, blinking skull flashlights, and garbage bag capes, then hollered back toward the car, "Good grief, Linda! What are these costumes supposed to be?"

Linda Joyce yelled back, "My daddy died! They had to come to his funeral instead of going to Disney World. There was nothing left at the store except that stuff. They're vampire mice! Now shut up and give 'em some candy!"

This scenario played out on the front porch of pretty much every house we visited. I don't know if people felt sorry for the poor little vampire mice or feared Linda Joyce, but either way, we collected a huge haul of Halloween treats.

We went back to our home in Kentucky and settled into the old familiar routine including Wednesday night prayer services. I still really wanted to go to Disney World, and when I was about ten years old I learned a new way to express that desire of my heart within the bounds of spiritual decorum. I knew my dad had kind of been mulling over in his mind whether we should try again for Disney World. So, I sort of pushed the envelope by raising my hand during the prayer meeting at church and saying, "My family has an important decision to make. And also, we would covet your prayers for traveling mercies." I had adapted the phrase "traveling mercies" to my own purpose. It's actually a Baptist's desperate cry for help flung up to heaven as they drive through rush hour traffic on the interstate in Atlanta.

It must have worked, because the very next day my dad said, "Let's try the trip to Disney World again."

Yes! There was still a God and He still loved me!

My sister and I were older now and we no longer played *"Emergency!"* on long road trips. Plus, we had traded in our Ford Pinto station wagon for a dark green Buick. That car was perfect for boogering people.

You may not be familiar. Let me explain.

First, you write this message on a piece of paper: "If you get any closer to my back bumper, I'll flick a booger on your windshield." Next, you post the sign in the back window of your car. Then you give everyone in the automobile, even the driver, a tissue. Finally, everybody pokes a corner of their tissue up their nose so it is hanging from one nostril. When all of that is in place, the driver slows the car so people coming up from behind are forced to pass and will inevitably read the sign posted in the back window. As they drive by, everybody with a tissue hanging out of their nose stares out the window at the people in the other car. Laughter ensues!

We were going to have crazy fun boogering people all the way to Orlando. But the week of our trip, the phone rang. My mama hung up the receiver and said, "Uncle Ralph died."

Which was a mercy from the Lord, because if he had not died, I probably would have killed him myself! We did not go to Orlando to visit the Magic Kingdom. We went to Alabama. You know what they have in Alabama? Pretty much the same thing as Mississippi, only worse, because Uncle Ralph and Aunt Nina did not have any children. There was no cool cousin to drive us around in her big car and show us a fun time.

Now I don't want you to think I was mad at Aunt Nina. No, not at all. It certainly wasn't her fault that her husband's untimely death resulted in a second cancellation of our trip to Disney World. We loved Aunt Nina. She was the matriarch of our family, a very sophisticated and fashionable lady of the Old South. But bless her heart, her hairline had begun to recede. To compensate, she would pluck out her eyebrows, then paint them back on in high arches. This was an attempt to raise the top of her face and minimize her ever-expanding forehead. The further her hairline receded, the higher she painted the eyebrows. It caused her to look as if she was in a perpetual state of shock.

The day after Uncle Ralph's funeral she called me into his library. Uncle Ralph was an avid reader with a large collection of beautifully bound volumes. Aunt Nina was holding a small book in her hand. "I'm very sorry your trip to the theme park was cancelled."

I said, "Yes, ma'am. That's all right."

She smiled. "You are a very polite boy. I know it was disappointing and this might not be much of a consolation, but I would like you to have this book. A friend of ours wrote it and perhaps when you come to visit on a happier occasion we can ask Nelle Harper Lee to sign your personal copy of her novel, *To Kill a Mockingbird*."

I was ten years old and it was some time before I actually read the treasured volume Aunt Nina had given me. When I did read it, well, let's just say I learned much about the bitter disappointments other people had endured. By comparison, my twice-cancelled trip to Disney World was really nothing.

However, that did not change the fact that I still desperately wanted to go! When I was about fourteen years old and full of teenage angst, I heard one of those Baptist ladies utter that familiar platitude, "The Lord will give you the desire of your heart."

I just snapped. When it was time for prayer requests I stated without apology, "I want to go to Disney World!"

And that's probably what caused my grandpa to die. Seriously! Son of a ... preacher man! And the hard rub of the situation was that my grandpa had retired to south Florida. We were going to drive right through Orlando on our way to yet another funeral! Fully convinced the whole thing was a myth, I became a non-believer. There was no Magic Kingdom; nobody had actually ever seen Mickey Mouse!

We no longer had the Buick. Now we had a Ford Aerostar minivan. There ain't nothing cool about a minivan. On the long drive to my grandfather's funeral, I sat in the very back seat of that stupid minivan with my Sony Walkman cassette player. With the headset jammed down over my ears I blocked out everything around me. I had made myself a mixed tape labeled "Songs of Hope and Deliverance." But that was just for my Baptist preacher dad who was unaware I had recently become an atheist. I was actually rocking out my anger with Alice Cooper and Twisted Sister!

Just south of Atlanta we ran over something in the road, and the right back tire started rapidly deflating. My dad pulled over into the emergency lane. He motioned for me to take off my headphones. I begrudgingly climbed out of the car to help change the flat. We had the minivan up on a jack and were struggling to get the wheel off when a big clap of thunder came out of nowhere and rain began pouring out of the sky. My poor dad had had just about all he could take. When Uncle Ralph and Uncle Bill died, my dad being a minister, helped officiate their funerals. But this was his own father who had just passed away. My dad sat down in the mud and started to cry. I didn't know what else to do, so I just sat down in the mud and cried with him. After a few minutes we were able to change the tire. We got some towels out of our luggage, did our best to clean ourselves up, and drove on to Florida to bury my grandfather.

Five or six days later we were ready to make the return trip. I wasn't quite so angry anymore, but I was still pretty quiet around my dad. As we were driving north he said, "We don't have the time or money to stop at Disney World, but maybe we can have a picnic lunch at Tomoka State Park. I know how much you love American Indian lore. I read about a statue there you might like to see."

It was true I was very interested in Native American history and culture, but I really wasn't in the mood. I sat in the backseat thinking up a souvenir t-shirt that read, "My grandpa died and all I got was a trip to 'Camp Old Indian.'"

A couple hours later, we pulled into the park where we discovered not one, but several statues arranged in a sort of diorama. The tale is a complete myth, but as the story goes there was a brave warrior princess who fought against a treacherous chief named Tomoka. Looking at the statue, one must conclude she fought her battles completely in the nude. Well, I was already a fourteen-year-old Baptist turned atheist expressing rebellion with rock and roll music. Needless to say, the longer I stared at that statue the more concerned my dad became. Consequently, when I graduated from high school, he made me attend the Christian Fundamentalist school, Bob Jones University!

When I graduated from college my dad said, "Before you settle into a job, I think you deserve to go on a trip. Some kids backpack through Europe. Others choose to visit the Grand Canyon. Where would you like to go?"

I was shocked he even had to ask. "I want to go you-know-where, but before I plan my trip, I want you and mom to see the doctor for complete physicals with full blood panels."

My dad laughed. "I understand your concern. It's true your mother and I aren't as young as we used to be, but neither are you. So we aren't going to take you to Disney World. We're giving you money to rent a van and you can take a bunch of your college buddies."

My college graduation trip consisted of six Bob Jones boys driving to Orlando, Florida in a rental van to cut loose in the Magic Kingdom. On the return drive I began telling stories about my lifelong quest to get to Disney World. I was surprised to learn my friends had never played *"Emergency!"* in the back of a Ford Pinto station wagon. They had never boogered passing cars from the backseat of a Buick. I remedied that situation by making a sign and passing out tissues. They thought that activity was just about as fun as anything we had experienced in the park.

I began to realize that even though most of my friends had been to Disney World lots of times, they had grown up poor. They had suffered deprived childhoods. And in that moment my faith was fully restored to me as I thought, *The Lord has given me the desire of my heart. My cup runneth over. Surely goodness and mercy shall follow me all the days of my life. I shall not return unto the Magic Kingdom but will cherish childhood memories, not to mention an autographed copy of Nelle Harper Lee's* To Kill a Mockingbird, *forever.*

THANKS, TEACH

I will be forever grateful to my teachers. There is not a Hallmark card big enough to express my gratitude. From first grade all the way to my high school graduation ceremony, my school career was one colorful experience after another, largely because of my teachers. And my bus driver, Mr. Minx.

Mr. Minx provided a marvelous introduction to everything that was to follow. As a six-year-old, I was excited to attend school, but the excitement was more for the school bus than anything else. Kindergarten was only available for children who lived in town and attended the city school. I would be starting in first grade, without any preview or orientation. I didn't really know what to expect in the classroom, but I had seen the big, yellow school bus go by my house many times. The idea of riding on that bus, all by myself, was thrilling.

On the very first day of my school career, I was out by the roadside plenty early. I clutched a canvas book bag that buckled with two straps down the front in one hand and my Peanuts lunchbox with pictures of Charlie Brown and Snoopy in the other. I'm sure my mom was watching from the front room window, but I felt quite grown up to be standing by the road without an adult. When the big bus pulled up and came to a stop I thrilled to the sound of the air brakes letting off pressure. *Psssht!* The door swung open to reveal three great big steps. I knew I was about to embark on a great adventure.

I was so little I couldn't even get up the first step. I had to fling my lunchbox in, fling my book bag in, and then crawl up onto the landing. The other steps were easier. After I had picked up my book bag and lunchbox, I straightened up and saw the whole bus was empty. I was the very first stop.

The bus driver looked at me and said, "Oh, I am so glad a big, capable boy like you is my first passenger. I'm going to need your help."

Then he held up his right arm, which was encased in a plaster cast that started at his knuckles and went all the way up to his shoulder. The hard plaster held his elbow at a ninety-degree angle. I later learned just about a week before school started he had fallen and broken his arm. I don't know if there wasn't a substitute driver available or if he was desperate to keep the job, but it was obvious that shifting gears was more than a little difficult with his arm in a cast.

The bus driver said, "I'm Mr. Minx. What's your name?"

I lay my book bag and lunchbox in a seat, as I answered, "My name is Tim Lowry."

"Well Timmy Lowry, you're going to learn how to drive a stick shift." He immediately began the lesson. "You stand right here next to me and hold onto this big stick. Do you know your letters?"

"Yes, sir."

"Good. There's a little picture right here on the top of this stick. It looks kind of like the letter H with an extra hitchick for reverse, but you don't need to worry about that. Here's what we're going to do. You hold onto this stick and I'm going to mash in this pedal called the clutch. When I'm mashing in this pedal, I'll say 'go,' and you pull the stick straight down. That'll be second gear. Then when I say 'go' again, you push up and over into third gear. Then when we get going pretty fast and you hear the engine whine, I'll mash in the clutch and you pull it down into fourth. Can you do that?"

I shouted excitedly, "Yes, sir!"

And away we went with the school bus lurching along as I stood next to the driver shifting gears. We had a little grinding, but for the most part it went pretty smoothly. We arrived safely at school with a busload of kids and all the boys begging to take my job. That afternoon, on the return trip home, Mr. Minx let another boy help. Several of us boys took turns shifting gears for six weeks until he had his cast removed.

✵✵✵

At Rosspoint Elementary School in Harlan County, Kentucky, there were five classrooms spaced along a single hallway with a cafeteria at the end. Our library was in one corner of the cafeteria. It consisted of four bookshelves, two on one wall and two on the other, and a big square rug on the floor in between. Twice a week, a lady with a mustache named Mrs. Howard came to help us select books from those shelves to check out and take home.

Right next to the cafeteria/library was my first grade classroom. My teacher was Mrs. Wilder. I'm sure my mom and dad had met her at "Meet the Teacher Night" a day or two before, but I didn't know what I was in for. Mrs. Wilder was the most interesting person I had ever met. She kept everything needed for teaching school on her person, kind of like a cowboy. You know how a cowboy has guns hanging from his belt so he can shoot a bad guy, and a hat for shading his face when he takes a nap, and a pair of boots for kicking rattlesnakes? That was Mrs. Wilder. She had everything she needed for educating the youth of Southeastern Kentucky on her body. She didn't carry a purse. She didn't carry a book bag. She tucked all the tools needed for teaching first grade "down there," beneath her blouse, close to her heart.

She kept money down there. If you went to the cafeteria and had forgotten your lunch money, that was a big problem, because the lady in the hairnet who ran the cash register was going to fuss at you. But Mrs. Wilder would come to the rescue. "What's the matter, honey? Did you forget your lunch money?" Then she would reach in and pull out a dollar bill and hand it to you. School lunch was thirty-five cents in those days, so there was change. She dropped the coins down there and they didn't even jingle! She kept makeup down there, a compact tucked into one side and a tube of lipstick in the other. After she finished her lunch, she would reach in and perform a kind of cross-draw to pull them out. Using the mirror in the compact, she would put on a little lipstick, then tuck those items back into their respective places. She kept a spoon down there. But not for the cafeteria. No, the spoon was for reading class.

I learned to read with three friends. If you're of a certain age, they were probably your friends too. Dick, Jane, and Spot. I use the term "friends" very loosely, because we actually hated Dick and Jane and their dog Spot. They lived the most boring lives ever.

Chapter One: See Dick run. Run, Dick, run.
Chapter Two: See Jane run. Run, Jane, run.
Chapter Three: See Spot run. Run, Spot, run.

The book was so monotonous you couldn't help but lean over and talk to your neighbor when it was somebody else's turn to read. I still remember when my buddy Todd leaned over and whispered to me, "Get hit with a car, Spot! Die, Spot, die!" I suppose that's what happened, because in second grade Dick and Jane got a new dog named Lad.

Now if you were talking to your neighbor when you were supposed to be reading about Dick, Jane, and Spot,

Mrs. Wilder would always catch you. We never could fig-ure out how she knew we were whispering. We tried to be so quiet, but it didn't work. You would hear her chair scrape against the floor as she pushed back and stood up from behind her desk. Then you would hear her hard-soled shoes clomping on the wooden floor as she walked across the room toward you. Shocked that you had been caught, you would look up at her with your mouth gaping open. That's when she would pull out that spoon, wipe it on the hem of her dress, and say, "Does your tongue need something to do? Here, suck on this for a while!" Then she would poke that spoon right into your open mouth, and you did not dare remove it until she said to remove it.

Many a kid would go home on the big, yellow school bus to complain to their mama. But nobody's mama ever called the school board threatening to sue. If a kid said, "Mrs. Wilder stuck a spoon in my mouth today," every mama in Harlan County replied, "Of course she did. You were probably talking to your neighbor when you were supposed to be reading about Dick, Jane, and Spot." If the kid asked, "How did you know?" the mom would answer, "Because she stuck a spoon in my mouth when I was in first grade." Everybody in Harlan County had been spooned by Mrs. Wilder at least once or twice. That's how we learned to read.

If you talked during reading class, it was the spoon, but if you talked during math class, Mrs. Wilder had an entirely different punishment. First, she would move you away from your friends by taking hold of the front of your little desk and, with you still sitting in the seat, sliding it across the room. When she bent over your desk, you could see "down there." That alone was punishment enough, but I don't think anyone ever made her aware. You would end up with your desk facing the great big triple-sash windows lining the outside wall of the classroom.

Man, those windows were dangerous. They were outfitted with chains running up and down the long edges with little weights hanging from them. The mechanism was a counterbalance for raising up the heavy sash. If those weights fell off the end of the chain, the balance went out of whack and the window sash would come crashing down. I remember one time in fourth grade when a boy got his finger chopped off by the falling window sash. It was the pencil sharpener's fault. The school had switched from hand crank to electric pencil sharpeners. We were fascinated. This boy kept going up to the new electric pencil sharpener and running his pencil down. One day while he was standing at the pencil sharpener, he absent-mindedly laid a hand on the sill of the open window. Without warning the sash came crashing down and chopped the end of his middle finger right off. The tip of his finger flew out into the school yard. My friend Todd jumped up and yelled, "I know what to do. You should put it in milk!" (Actually, I think that's what you do if someone gets a tooth knocked out, but we discovered it also works for a finger.) Todd ran to the cafeteria/library and grabbed a carton of milk. The principal stuck that boy's fingertip into the milk and took him to the emergency room where they sewed it back on.

I digress. That was in fourth grade, I'm supposed to be talking about first grade.

If you interrupted math class, Mrs. Wilder would pull your desk over to the windows and point to a tree on the playground.

"Do you see that oak tree out there on the playground?"

"Yes, ma'am."

"In fifteen minutes I'm going to ask you how many leaves are on that oak tree. If you don't have the right number ... well, you're going to wish you did!"

We believed she knew the total number because there was a plaque on the trunk of the tree stating she had planted it on Arbor Day in 1957. Of course, our efforts to count leaves on a tree always ended in tears, because school starts in the fall. The wind would blow and leaves would fall off, causing us to lose count.

She would say, "See there! You can't even subtract a few leaves from the total number on a tree. That's why you need to study mathematics. Now bring your desk back over here and pay attention."

One day my friend Todd was moved to count leaves on the tree. "I know how many leaves are on that tree because my brother Spencer was in first grade last year, and he already told me."

It didn't work. You could never get ahead of Mrs. Wilder. She shot back, "No, that's not true. Every winter they fall off and in the spring God puts on a new number that He only tells me. So you better start counting."

✥✥✥

Mrs. Wilder never missed anything you might be up to, and you couldn't get away from her; she was everywhere. She even rode the big, yellow school bus. We heard her reason with the bus driver, "Why pay for gasoline when you'll take me to work for free?" Consequently, Mrs. Wilder never had to stay for faculty meetings. The principal would stop by the classroom to remind her of an after-school meeting and she would say, "I can't stay. The bus is my ride. Gotta go." The principal never argued because she had been his teacher when he was in first grade.

Mrs. Wilder lived in a big old Victorian house way up on a hill overlooking the road. She was the first drop-off in the afternoon, and in the mornings, she was the last person to be picked up. Our driver, Mr. Minx, would drive right up the hill to turn around in her driveway, so she only had to walk a few steps from her front porch to the bus. One winter morning, he could not get up the hill. Some water had trickled down her driveway and frozen the night before to form a solid sheet of ice.

Mr. Minx opened the bus door and called up the hill, "Mrs. Wilder, I can't come up there and get you. It's too slick."

"Wait, wait, wait! I can't miss school." She disappeared around the corner of her house and quickly returned with a cardboard box. She ripped that box open to fashion a sled, sat down on it and came flying down the hill. *Whoosh!* She stood up, tossed the cardboard into the weeds, and climbed onto the bus. We all cheered and clapped. She put one hand to her heart and we fell silent, fearing the spoon would make an appearance due to our rowdiness.

All of us elementary kids loved visiting Mrs. Wilder's house at Halloween for trick-or-treating. She would tease us by handing out gag gifts instead of candy. One year she gave every kid a ping pong ball. Another year she handed out raw potatoes. Always a surprise. She played with us in the classroom too, especially when she read from "The Big Book." Mrs. Wilder always reserved the last half-hour of each Friday for what she called "Big Book Time." She invited us to leave our seats and sit on a rug in front of a rocking chair in one corner of the classroom. Then she would choose one person for the special task of going to her desk to fetch "The Big Book." If Mrs. Wilder chose you, it was a big deal. The book was obviously very old. The spine was cracked and the gold edging on the pages was all but worn away. It was a weighty, venerable tome. We figured whatever had not been recorded in the Bible was written upon the pages of "The Big Book."

Actually, it was a complete anthology of fairytales. The Brothers Grimm. Charles Perrault. Hans Christian Andersen. Russian stories from Pushkin. Tales of the Arabian Nights. As Mrs. Wilder read aloud from "The Big Book," the rug beneath us became a magic carpet on which we flew away to places only Peter Pan had ever visited. She did voices and acted out exciting parts. We were mesmerized. We especially liked The Brothers Grimm, because she read us the whole story, even the gory parts. Did you know one of Cinderella's stepsisters used a butcher knife to chop off her own toes trying to fit her big, ugly foot into the tiny glass slipper? And The Three Bears does not end with Goldilocks running away. Oh no! The ending Mrs. Wilder read to us was much more delicious than that—especially for the three bears! I could have stayed in first grade for another whole year, but alas, we first graders grew up into second graders.

Second grade was just a blur. We learned cursive writing; all those letters linking together with loopity loops! Mrs. Estes, my second-grade teacher, posted a series of charts across the top of our blackboard shaped like Conestoga wagons following one another along the Oregon Trail. Each wagon had a cursive letter written on its expansive white canvas. The A wagon linked to the B wagon. The B wagon linked to the C wagon. Every afternoon, Mrs. Estes would have us copy those letters over and over, linking A, B, C, and so forth with the loopity loops she was able to draw so effortlessly. I was never very good at cursive writing. Watching her glide her hand across the blackboard was like watching a figure skater on the ice. All that twirling made me dizzy.

Then came third grade, with a teacher fresh out of college. Miss Clem was very progressive. She hung a mirror ball in the back of her classroom and taught us our multiplication tables with disco. An eight-track tape player cranked out the soundtrack from the hit movie *Saturday Night Fever*. As we learned to dance like John Travolta, we recited our multiplication tables to the beat. "Two times two is—*boom thump*—four! Two times four is—*boom thump*—eight! Two times eight is—*boom thump*—sixteen! Sixteen twice is—*thump, thump, thump, thump*—thirty-two!" It was terrific.

If you missed one, Miss Clem would teach you a dance called "The Bump" and knock you off the dance floor. Then you had to sit down until the song was over. Disco math was way more fun than filling in multiplication tables. To this day I still can't do simple math in my head unless I get a good beat going.

My fourth-grade teacher was a force of nature named Pauline Wilson, the chain-smoking daughter of a thrice-dunking Baptist preacher. I suppose Mrs. Wilson was the way she was because she had been baptized by her daddy. When he took you "down to the river to pray" he dunked you under once for the Father, again for the Son, and a third time for the Holy Spirit. By the time he was finished you had been under water for a good long while. I don't know if all that dunking and holding your breath made folks better Christians, but it made a man out of Pauline Wilson. She was tough!

With her bright red fingernail polish and Virginia Slim cigarettes, Pauline Wilson reminded you more of a dragon than a schoolteacher. She had two favorite subjects: fractions and the Apocalypse. And if you weren't successful with the former, then you would suffer the latter. We hated it when she gave us a fractions test, so we would do our best to use her love of the Apocalypse to distract her from mathematics. I was in fourth grade during the height of the Cold War. Everybody was talking about the threat of nuclear holocaust. We saw reports about the arms race between the United States and Russia on the evening news. If we saw Mrs. Wilson getting ready to walk down the hall to the teacher's lounge, we knew she was going to run off dreaded fractions test pages on the ditto machine.

Ah, the ditto machine! That dynamo of a duplicator that produced the damp pages covered in purple ink. I remember lifting the pages to my face to smell them, then going home at the end of the school day with a purple dot on the end of my nose. That's why there was such a drug problem in the 1980s; a decade earlier we kids were snorting purple ditto pages. Just say no to ditto!

Anyway— to keep Mrs. Wilson away from the ditto machine, we would bring up current events. Somebody would say, "Mrs. Wilson, in social studies this morning I forgot to mention what I saw on the news last night. Walter

Cronkite said ..." And that was as far as you ever got, because she would stop walking toward the classroom door, spin around, and deliver an impassioned speech.

"Oh, children! I watched the news last night. Everybody's got missiles. There are missiles in secret silos all over the place. You know what the Bible says, 'Not by water, but next time by fire!' My daddy is a Baptist preacher and I know all about this stuff. Russia is the bear. China is the dragon. It's all in the Book of Revelation. One of these days somebody is going to push a big red button and boom! Vaporized. We're all going to be vaporized. There won't be anything left!"

Mrs. Wilson would get herself so worked up that she would be in desperate need of a cigarette. She would cancel the fractions test and let us go out on the playground for a little extra recess while she went to the teacher's lounge to smoke. That room always smelled like ditto ink and tobacco because Mrs. Wilson was so worried about fractions and the Apocalypse. Sometimes she would send one of us students across the road to the convenience store to buy cigarettes for her. She would get into her pocketbook and take out money as she gave specific instructions. "Go across to the store and get me a pack of Virginia Slims. Tell them it's for me, and they'll sell them to you. I also want a Tab soda. Buy yourself a little treat with the change."

One day, she gave me the money and sent me to get the cigarettes and the diet soda in the pink can. I thought,

"Hmm, Mrs. Wilson drinks that pink pop. I think I'll try one." Yuck! One swallow of that saccharine-sweetened stuff and I decided it was better to try a cigarette! Don't worry. I didn't take up smoking in the fourth grade. It was just a thought.

However, my friends and I did take the Apocalypse seriously. During recess we'd hold meetings while sitting on top of the monkey bars to try and figure out a plan in case the Russians landed while we were at school. Familiar with World War II movies that had paratroopers jumping out of airplanes, we figured it'd be something like that. Enemy soldiers falling out of the sky all over the playground. One day this boy named Jeff said, "I know exactly what we'll do. I've got it all worked out. At the end of the hallway there's the cafeteria. Across from the bookshelves, on the other side of the room there's a door with a big, red sign that says, 'Do not open. Alarm will sound.' When the Russians land, we're gonna run down the hallway, go through the cafeteria, bust that door open, the alarm will go off, and that'll call the police and let them know the Apocalypse has started."

Somebody said, "But we'll still get killed."

Jeff countered, "No we won't because we can run down the road and up the hill to Mrs. Wilder's house and jump 'down there!'" We figured that was a good plan, because close to our first-grade teacher's heart was certainly a place where the Russians would dare not go!

✳✳✳

I could talk all day about my teachers. I remember every single one. My fifth-grade teacher, Mr. Orby Hunley, played the banjo and taught us how to square dance. I had a seventh-grade teacher, Mrs. Simpson, who sponsored bubble-gum-blowing contests during study hall. There was an eighth-grade Advanced Studies teacher who was very short. We called him Brainy Smurf. All of those elementary and junior high adventures took place in smaller, country schools, but for high school all of us country kids were bussed to the huge, consolidated school. I remember when the entire student body of more than 1500 kids assembled in the gym on the first day of high school. The principal stepped up to the microphone and called for the freshman class to stand. All the upperclassmen booed and cat-called, some threw paper wads. The first few weeks of high school would have been overwhelming without Mrs. Amy Wills. She was our freshman English teacher.

Mrs. Wills had grown up a country kid and she had a soft spot for all of us who came from the far end of the county. At the beginning of the year, she announced we would read her favorite play aloud, William Shakespeare's *Romeo and Juliet*. We were nervous. Shakespeare? Wasn't that pretty hard? What if we mispronounced stuff and everybody laughed?

We didn't know it, but Mrs. Amy Wills was the sister of our first-grade teacher, Mrs. Wilder, and they used some of the same teaching methods; not the spoon, but other things were very familiar. On the day we started *Romeo and Juliet*, Mrs. Wills invited us all to come sit on a rug in front of a rocking chair. Then she asked a student to bring from her desk *The Collected Works of William Shakespeare*. As we sat at her feet, she read the play aloud from the big book. She used different voices for all the characters and encouraged us to act out the most exciting scenes. We all took a pencil and she showed us how to hold a sword for the duel between Tybalt and Mercutio. It took a full week to read the five-act play, a single act each day. She was really into it; by week's end so were we. Mrs. Wills even cried when Romeo, then Juliet committed suicide. But we didn't find that display of emotion the least bit strange or weird, because Mrs. Amy Wills was playing with us, just like Mrs. Wilder used to do. The story was different, the subject matter more serious, but nonetheless magical. We knew Mrs. Wills kept not only Romeo and Juliet, but also us students, close to her heart.

✣✣✣

I began by stating there isn't a Hallmark card big enough to express my gratitude to my teachers. Instead, I will reference a story. This story is not from the Brothers Grimm or William Shakespeare, but comes from THE big book which speaks of a teacher who was also a healer. One day the teacher stopped along a roadside to heal a group of poor lepers. After he had performed this miracle, they all ran away rejoicing. Only one of those poor lepers returned to thank the teacher. Interestingly enough, it is written that this one was a Samaritan, a country kid from the far end of the county, so to speak. I think being a teacher is a lot like that story. Over the course of their careers, teachers meet many students and always do their best to not only fill their heads but also inspire their hearts. Most of those students go off to live their lives and the teachers never see them again. They don't mean to seem ungrateful for the magic that was shared. It's just that life goes on, one thing leading to another, making it hard, sometimes impossible, for them to return. So please allow me to be the one representing the many, as I say thank you to teachers everywhere. Thank you for keeping us close to your heart.

STAY ON THE ROAD

I graduated from college with a bachelor's degree in Speech and Drama, plus a teaching credential for English Language Arts. Both of these things would ultimately prove invaluable to my career as a professional storyteller, but right after college I was living with my parents because the only job I could find was at McDonald's. Fast food was certainly not my ambition, but the path leading to professional storytelling was unclear.

I decided to take a road trip because I do my best thinking in the car. One of my college classmates was from Charleston, South Carolina, so I drove toward the coast to visit him and figure things out along the way. Because there's never anything interesting to see along an interstate, I chose an alternative route on a country road where I saw all kinds of interesting things. There was a cow. Then another cow. After that ... a cow. Finally, the monotony was broken when I spied a camel. At first I wasn't sure. I was driving along at a good clip, and whatever I saw went by pretty fast. It might have just been an old, arthritic horse. I came upon a little country church with a gravel parking lot and took that as a sign. "Let us turn aside and see this thing which has come to pass."

I turned around in the church parking lot and drove back. Sure enough, alongside the road, standing behind three strands of barbed wire, was a dromedary camel chewing on a mouthful of weeds and looking at me from beneath droopy eyelids as if to say, "So what?" I noticed a hand-painted sign next to the fence that read "O'Cain's Wild Animal Park" with an arrow pointing up a dirt road. Well, of course I had to investigate further! I turned onto the dirt lane which led to a modest, brick ranch with a parking area off to one side. I parked my car and stepped out to see a gentleman approaching me on a riding lawn mower pulling a small trailer. The trailer was full of what was obviously discarded produce from the local Piggly Wiggly: wilted heads of lettuce, a few small potatoes, some carrots, and an eggplant past its prime.

The gentleman turned off the mower and asked, "You want to see my zoo?"

I assumed I was talking to Mr. O'Cain himself. "Well, my curiosity got the better of me when I saw your camel by the side of the road."

He started up the mower. "It'll cost you four dollars to ride with me."

What a deal! I took four one-dollar bills out of my wallet and handed them over. He stuffed the money into his shirt pocket and instructed me to climb on behind him. He put the thing in gear and we were off on our safari.

Mr. O'Cain drove me out to the edge of a wide, grassy field. He turned off the engine and said, "Just wait a minute."

It took just about that much time for a prairie dog to pop up from a hole in the ground. It sort of barked and another one popped up from a different place. Pretty soon prairie dogs were popping up all over. I must have counted more than twenty. Mr. O'Cain explained the first one was the lookout signaling the "all clear" after determining we weren't deadly predators. I had never seen anything more fascinating and entertaining.

I asked, "How in the world did you get a prairie dog town in South Carolina?"

"Did you go to school? I mean like college."

I answered in the affirmative.

"Well they didn't teach you very much. This ain't rocket science. You get a male prairie dog and a female prairie dog, dig a hole, throw them down in there, and come spring—Boom! Prairie dog town!" He followed up his concise biology lesson with "Now I'll let you feed my ostrich."

He fired up the lawn mower and we drove a little distance to a different area surrounded by tall fencing. He hopped off the mower and snatched a carrot out of the trailer, handed it to me, and pointed to a giant bird towering over the fence. I reached up and the ostrich bobbed its head down, snatched the carrot, and swallowed it whole. You would think a bird with such a long, skinny throat would gulp a carrot down lengthwise, but it was turned sideways. I could see the outline of that carrot traveling down its neck as the ostrich struggled to swallow.

I laughed as Mr. O'Cain said, "They're not the brightest birds. Pretty much a chicken on steroids." My laughter was cut short when my host announced, "Now I want to show you my snake house."

I thought, *that sounds nasty*. Well, it pretty much was.

We drove over to a little barn, one of those sheds like you buy at Lowe's or Home Depot for backyard storage. He hopped off the mower and started working a combination on a giant padlock hanging from a hasp on the front door. When he flung the door open, I was still sitting on the mower, not planning to make one move toward that shed. From my vantage point I could see it was all fixed up like a jungle room with scenes painted on the walls and potted plants scattered all around. There was even a water feature. I could also plainly see more than one giant snake slithering across the floor, which prompted me to say, "I'm not going in there."

"They won't hurt you."

"I know they won't, because I'm not going in there."

He closed the snake house door and fastened the lock. Returning to the mower he said, "Well, if you don't like snakes I won't insist, but when we come to the alligator pit I won't take 'no' for an answer."

On our way over to the alligator pit we drove past a family of raccoons living in a hollow tree and paused long enough at the marsupial pen for me to be quickly educated on the difference between a wallaby and a kangaroo. When we passed by my old friend the camel, I saw he shared a pasture with several llamas, a burro, and some sort of African cow with ridiculously long horns. Finally, we arrived at the alligator pit, which was actually a large pond surrounded by an eight-foot chain-link fence with barbed-wire running around the top. The setup looked more like a reptile prison yard than a zoo enclosure, although I will say it was a very beautifully appointed prison yard. The water looked clean. There were plants all around and a large wooden platform floating in the middle of the pond.

Mr. O'Cain turned off the engine of the riding mower with instructions for me to follow. He walked over to a tall gate that was securely fastened with a huge padlock and chain. Unlocking the gate and swinging it open he declared, "I got ten alligators in here. Come on in and I'll introduce you."

By that point, I was kind of in a daze, this whole experience being rather surreal. I did not protest. However, I did have enough wits about myself to take stock of the situation. Glancing all around the pond I saw an alligator's head sticking up out of the water. A couple more were sunning themselves atop the floating platform, and several more lay on the far bank. I started counting gators. *One, two, three, four, five, six, seven, eight, nine.* I checked my math by counting again, only backwards. *Nine, eight, seven, six, five, four, three, two, one.* I began to get a little nervous.

Looking behind myself, I asked, "Didn't you tell me you had ten alligators in here?"

"Oh yeah, that's the total. Number ten is a mama with babies."

"I've heard about that. You don't mess with a mama alligator's babies."

He reassured me by saying, "No, no, it's all right. The weather is pretty cool today and their blood isn't pumping really good yet. They can't move too fast. She's dug herself a hole in this bank here by the side of the pond." Then he shifted into sort of a carnival barker's voice as he added with a grand gesture, "If you want to see a mama alligator and her babies, all you have to do is just grab a hold of this sapling tree. Then kind of swing down and look back in that hole. She'll come crawling out and you can see the babies walking around on her head and riding on her back." I just stood there, frozen, so he added, "It'll be fine. You'll hear her bellow and that's when you know it's time to climb back up the bank."

I did it! I grabbed hold of the sapling and swung down. Sure enough, I was looking at an eight-foot alligator and her children! But it didn't seem dangerous. It was like I was having an out-of-body experience. She made sort of a low rumbling sound and I suddenly realized exactly what I was doing. I scrambled back up the bank and said, "Well, it's getting late, I better go!"

Mr. O'Cain drove me back to my car. I thanked him for the tour and asked, "How did you end up with a backyard full of exotic animals?"

He was rather serious when he answered. "When I was a kid all I ever wanted to be was a zoologist. But my daddy said, 'There ain't no money in that. You're going to work construction just like me.' My daddy was a strong, tough man, and I was afraid to cross him. So I took over his construction business for thirty-five years. I hated it, but I saved all my money and when I retired, I bought myself a zoo." He took me by both shoulders and looked me dead in the eye.

"Son, don't wait thirty-five years to do what you really want to do."

I still had some distance to drive and more time for thinking, but my decision was made. After visiting my friend, I went back to my parents' house, quit my job at McDonald's, packed up my stuff, and moved to Charleston to follow my dream. When I told my friend I wanted to be a professional storyteller he said, "Uh, would you like fries with that?" But I was determined to go forward and never look back. With its beautiful historic district and a deeply rooted folk culture, Charleston was the perfect place to begin.

I signed on as a carriage-driving tour guide. Dressed in a cheap costume version of a Confederate uniform, I stood at the smelly end of a horse, pointing out sites of interest with a buggy whip and telling the Yankees, "This is this, and that is that." Like all the other carriage drivers, if I wasn't quite sure of the historic facts, I would just make stuff up, which gave me lots of experience in storytelling. It wasn't a performance career, but it was a start. However, I was as poor as Job's turkey. I lived on a low hourly wage plus tips. Every day was my birthday. (That's an old tour guide trick. You get a friend to wave to you from the street and yell, "Hey Tim! Happy birthday, man!" The tourists assume it's true and they tip extra.) Adding to my poverty, my fellow carriage drivers engaged in a little hazing. When I had completed my training and did my first solo tour, they fed my horse bananas, which gave him horrid gas. As I went rolling down the street trying to eke out a living, my horse was punctuating my sentences every step of the way. Tips were not so good that day.

I didn't have a car; I rode a bicycle back and forth to work. For extra money I hocked my high school class ring, then my college class ring. The only living space I could afford was no bigger than a sailor's berth on a cargo ship. My apartment was so small I could sit on the toilet and do dishes at the same time. I ate breakfast cereal for supper. Being entirely on my own was no picnic, and I was terribly homesick, but equally determined to not move back in with my parents.

One particular summer evening I had worked until about seven. Because it was so lonely at my apartment, I volunteered to stay late to help groom and feed the horses. Finally, I took my bicycle and started up Anson Street toward home. This route took me past St. John's Reformed Episcopal Church, a historic structure with no air conditioning. All the windows were open, allowing music from inside to float out into the dark, humid night. Hearing old hymns from my childhood, I stopped. Standing on the sidewalk listening to the singing made me more homesick than ever. I felt salty tears trickling down my cheeks and stinging my sunburnt face. Suddenly, I was aware of someone standing next to me. I turned to see a lady standing very close. She was dressed all in lavender and looked like an African queen. She wore a lavender hat that complimented her lavender suit, and a lavender silk blouse accessorized by a large lavender silk bow. She was also wearing lavender stockings and lavender high-heeled shoes. Next to her stood a little boy dressed in ... orange (I figured he was adopted).

The lady smiled and said, "Come inside and praise the Lord with us."

I felt embarrassed. "Oh, ma'am, I've been working at the carriage company all day. I smell horrible and I look worse. Hearing hymns that my mother sang to me as a child was a great blessing, but I can't come to a worship service dressed like this."

"God don't care how you look, as long as you show up. Now I can see you're moved, and I think you need this. I want you to come in. Just park your bicycle inside the gate by the door."

She was so gracious that I didn't need much persuading. Besides, after I leaned my bicycle against the gate, she stepped behind me and was formidable enough in stature to block any path of retreat.

I stepped from the dark street into the lit interior of St. John's Reformed Episcopal Church, which was built around 1850 as a chapel for enslaved Africans. Without thinking, I had entered this historic, sacred space dressed in a Confederate uniform. The singing stopped.

The pastor stood from his seat on the platform to announce, "We have a visitor." Then he stepped down to greet me with a handshake and asked if I would introduce myself to his congregation.

I have never been so awkwardly self-conscious in all my life! I managed to say my name was Tim and that I was new to Charleston.

The pastor assured me, "That's just fine. You're most welcome here. Please sit with your new friend."

Upon his invitation I sat in a pew with the lavender lady and her orange son as the pastor returned to the platform and the congregation continued singing. This was a special service commemorating the anniversary of the church's founding with music from a women's choir and a men's chorus in addition to the congregational singing. Then came time for the offering. Instead of passing a collection plate, all the children marched up front with money to put in a box on the communion table. I was not familiar with this tradition, but happy to contribute. I fished into my pocket to retrieve a five-dollar bill from my tour-guiding tips. I handed it to the little boy dressed in orange. He started to join the march, but his mama grabbed hold of his arm as she asked, "Where'd you get that money?"

He glanced toward me and said, "The white boy gave it to me." (Let me assure you. There was no question as to which white boy he was talking about!)

She told him to go ahead. He went up and put my money in the box. After the offering march, the men and women from the choir came down to sit in the pews with the rest of the congregation. It was time for the preaching.

I grew up a Baptist preacher's kid. I thought I knew what preaching was all about, but until that evening I had never heard preaching like that in my entire life! It was fabulous. First there was a reading from the Gospels. The preacher began, "Jesus was walking on the road ..." After this introductory statement he switched from English to Gullah, the seacoast island creole language spoken by enslaved Africans and their descendants. Reading from the Gullah translation of the New Testament, which was published by the American Bible Society, the preacher began again. "Dish yuh De Good Nyews Bout Jedus Christ Wa Luke Write."

The congregation responded, "Tank God fuh de Good Nyews."

I sat up to pay close attention. This was certainly different.

"Wiles Jedus an e ciple dem gone long de road, one man tell Jedus say, 'A gwine folla ya wehsoneba ya go.' Jedus ansa um say, 'De fox got hole een de groun, an de bod wa fly roun op een de air dey got nes. Bot de Man wa Come fom God ain got noweh fa lay e head.' Jedus tell noda man say, 'Come folla me!' Jedus tell all dem mans roun fuh come folla, but de ain gwine. So Jedus ansa um say, 'De poson wa staat fa plow groun an e keep on da look back hine em, e ain fit fuh lib onda God rule.'"

When the pastor finished the reading, he closed the book and spoke in English. "This concludes our reading from God's Holy Word."

The congregation responded, "Amen!"

His statement and the congregation's response had a finality about it, but he was just getting started. "This is a story about Jesus on the road. Ladies and gentlemen, I want you to turn to the person on your right and say, 'Get on the road.'"

We all turned to the person sitting next to us and said, "Get on the road."

Then he instructed, "Now turn to the person on your left and say, 'I said, get on the road!'"

Everyone turned in the opposite direction, repeating to our neighbor, "I said, get on the road!"

Now the preacher began to build. "You're on a road, ladies and gentlemen. You're on a journey with the Lord, and he's asking you to stay on the road with him. Do not get sidetracked, do not get distracted. Do not turn to the left. Do not turn aside to the right. Do not take the exit. Stay on the road!" Then he launched into the main part of his sermon. I was glad to be a visitor without any history in that place because he took no prisoners. He stopped just short of naming names. "Many of you are in danger of stepping off the road."

All of a sudden the organist, who was sitting with her hands poised over the keyboard, struck an ominous chord. I realized she was punctuating his sentences.

He spoke louder. "Stay on the road."

The congregation repeated, "Stay on the road."

The organist began to play as if she was pumping up the crowd at a Cincinnati Reds baseball game: *Bum, bum, bum, bum, bum, bum, bum, bum.*

The preacher's voice rose with the music. "You women come to me and say, 'Oh preacher, pray for me. God done close up my womb and I can't have no children.' So we pray and God performs a miracle and before you know it you got five children, but ain't none of them in Sunday School. I ask why these children are not attending the Sunday School. You say, 'Oh, I got one in diapers and one allergic to everything. I just don't know what I'm gonna do.' You women complain about the children God so graciously blessed you with. You take God's blessing and turn it into a curse! Get those children on the road to the church and the Sunday School. Get on the road!"

The congregation cried, "Get on the road!"

Then the preacher shouted, "And you men!"

All of a sudden the organist played the theme from Dragnet. *Da, da, da, da, dum!*

"You young men come to me saying, 'I ain't got no car.' We pray and get you a car. Then I don't see you no more. I say, 'Why ain't you in church?' And you say, 'Oh, I got to stay home and wash my car.' Get the car on the road to church! Get on the road!"

The congregation shouted back, "Get on the road!"

Now he was pushing toward a climax. The organist began laying down chords that started deep and low, then rose with the preacher's voice. "You may be trying hard to stay on the road. But it ain't easy following the Lord. You may feel down, you may feel weary, you may feel all by yourself."

"All by yourself." At that moment it seemed as if God was talking directly to me.

"But I am here to tell you, you are never alone. Never alone! The Holy Spirit is with you everywhere you go. He goes before you. He stands behind you. He walks beside you. We read from the Gullah Bible translated from the original Greek in which the Holy Spirit is known as the Paraclete. Let me put that down where you live. He is your parachute; he will catch you if you fall. He is your parasol; a shelter in the time of storm. He is your paralegal; he will defend you in a time of trial. He is your paratrooper; he will still the enemy and the avenger. He is your paramedic; he will save your sin-sick soul!"

The organist ended her long, slow build with a triumphant blast of sound as members of the congregation with hands in the air called out various responses. "Get on the road!" "Amen!" "Stay on the road!" "Yes, Lord!"

I never heard that much shouting in a church unless somebody had a snake! The shouts of praise and acclamation went on for a little while, but gradually everyone quieted back down when the preacher called out, "Whosonebeh betta heist de song!"

I later learned this traditional way of concluding a sermon had its origins back in slave times. Denied the opportunity for education, most enslaved African preachers were illiterate and untrained in sermon craft and delivery. After speaking for a while a preacher might not know how to finish. To spare the man of God an embarrassingly weak or feeble ending to his impassioned speech, the congregation would lift or "heist" a song to overwhelm the end of the sermon. Some people refer to this tradition as "singing the preacher down." I'm certain this pastor could have finished what he started, but he chose to end things the traditional way.

At last a white-haired gentleman I recognized from the men's chorus stood and began to sing without the organist's accompaniment.

"I'm just a poor wayfaring stranger,
A-traveling through this world of woe.
There's just a few more days to labor.
Before I fly to my heavenly home."

I knew that song. Black people sing it, but it's actually an Appalachian folk hymn from my childhood home in the mountains of Kentucky.

The rest of the congregation joined their voices with the old gentleman's, and we began filing out of the church to the sound of the a cappella hymn. We sang the last few words outside on the sidewalk. The service was concluded. The lavender lady stepped toward me with open arms. Her enthusiastic embrace was not a simple hug, she surrounded me completely.

Holding me close, she whispered in my ear. "Honey, if you miss your mama, then you come here to St. John's. Because here, you is family."

LEARNING STUFF

OUT'N NO BOOK

My momma and daddy wanted me to know as much as I could about the great big world beyond the Kentucky mountains where I was raised. So, they did what every other parent who wanted to broaden a boy's horizons would do—they purchased a set of *World Book Encyclopedias*. The twenty-two volumes were all lined up on the shelf beneath the hi-fi stereo, right next to the boxed sets of the 101 Strings Classical Orchestra and the Mormon Tabernacle Choir recordings of Handel's *Messiah*. My parents believed good books and good music went a long way in making a good boy.

My friend Britt's parents believed that too. They went even further and purchased not only a set of encyclopedias, but also subscribed to the *Childcraft* kids' book club. Approximately every six weeks a new book would arrive in the mail for Britt's collection. One summer afternoon, when my parents took my sister and me down to Britt's house for a playdate, he met us at the front door saying, "I got a new *Childcraft* all about Indians!" Five minutes later, the three of us were stretched out on our stomachs on his living room floor, paging through illustrated chapters about traditional Native American dress, songs, dances, food, and the types of homes they built. We were very inspired and decided to play Indian.

Britt's mom was happy to help us craft some quick costumes with her sewing scissors. By cutting the sleeves off some old shirts, she fashioned vests for us to wear. She also gave us an old lipstick to use as war paint, and we smeared stripes down the bridges of our noses and across our cheeks. From Britt's toy box we pulled out a plastic bow and several rubber-tipped arrows. We also found a certified hand-crafted weapon made by the Cherokee Indians—a throwing spear with a blunt, plastic head. We knew it was authentic because it had a paper tag attached that read "Certified hand-crafted weapon made by the Cherokee Indians."

(Years later, when I visited the Qualla Boundary reservation in North Carolina, I asked a Cherokee man about such toys. He laughingly said, "Oh sure, very authentic. The stick is made in Taiwan. The plastic spearhead comes from the Philippines. They ship them in separate crates. I stick them together with a little hot glue, add a few feathers, and tie that tag on before we sell them to white people like you.")

After we had gathered all our Indian stuff, Britt's mom said, "Now, go outside to play and don't come back in here."

My mom would've said the very same thing. That was another belief our parents had in common. Kids can't spend all their time looking at books, they need to go outside and get dirty.

Britt and I had no sooner hit the front porch than we ran into my sister standing on the steps. In our excitement we had forgotten about her, but there she was with one of those old shirt sleeves tied around her head with a couple feathers stuck into it and holding a baby doll.

She said, "I want to play."

"You're a girl."

"But I still want to play."

"You're still a girl."

"There were girl Indians!"

We couldn't argue with that. All three of us had studied the *Childcraft* book. There were girl Indians pictured on every other page.

"Fine, you can play." As we started walking toward the woods I announced, "We have to have Indian names. I will be Tall Man because I'm the biggest."

Britt enthusiastically replied, "Yeah, Tall Man!" Then he looked at my sister and said, "I can be Running Bear and you can be Little White Dove."

His inspiration didn't come from a physical trait or personality characteristic, but from singer Johnny Preston's ballad, "Running Bear," a song of teenage tragedy. We played his forty-five record all the time and sang along with the chorus about the star-crossed Indian lovers. It was very authentic. We could tell because of the background singers chanting, "Oogah chaka! Oogah chaka! Oogah chaka!" They sounded like real Indian words to us.

Everybody had an authentic Indian name until my sister announced Little White Dove's baby doll would be called Libby.

"No, that's not an Indian name," I scolded. "You have to call her something else."

"Libby is too an Indian name."

"Uh uh! You have to call her Cries A Lot or something like that."

"I'm not calling her that. She is my doll and I'm calling her Libby."

"If you aren't going to give her a real Indian name, you can't play with us."

"Oh yes, I can, because Britt's mom said 'Don't come back in here,' so I have to go with you. I am Libby's mommy so Libby is coming, too."

Dang! That was twice Little White Dove had made an unassailable argument. No wonder the Cherokee had a matriarchal society. It was settled. The tribe consisted of four members: Tall Man, Running Bear, Little White Dove, and Libby. (God has a sense of humor. I never dreamed I would grow up to become the father of adopted children. My older daughter is Native American. Her name is Libby.)

As soon as we arrived in the little patch of woods at the edge of Britt's backyard, we got to work building a tee-pee by propping a bunch of sticks all around the trunk of a pine tree. Crawling inside to inspect our shelter I proclaimed, "This is just like real Indians."

"No it's not," Britt contradicted. "I'm hungry. Real Indians had food."

"Well, let's go back to the house and get something to eat."

"You can't," Little White Dove interjected. "Britt's mom said, 'Don't come back in here.'"

I corrected my sister. "Don't call him Britt. We're playing Indians. His name is Running Bear."

"You know what I meant," retorted Little White Dove.

My sister and I were about to go on the warpath again when Running Bear proposed peace with a creative solution. "We can't go back inside, but maybe we can go to the door and offer my mom a trade."

We all agreed the plan had merit. Little White Dove stayed in the teepee while Running Bear and I went down to the creek to find some shiny white pebbles. With pretty rocks for trading, we went back to the house and knocked on the door.

As soon as she saw us standing there, Britt's mom started to fuss. "I told you boys—"

Britt interrupted. "We're not boys. We're full-blooded Cherokee Indians and we've come to trade."

Britt's mom smiled. "Alright Running Bear, whatcha got?"

He reached into a pocket and pulled out a handful of creek pebbles. "Oh, White Woman, we will trade you these beautiful stones for three Indian hotdogs."

White Woman held out for a better bargain. I tried to sweeten the deal with an additional offer. "I also have some string and a dead frog."

White Woman quickly sealed the deal by taking the stones and the string and allowing us to keep the frog. We waited on the front porch until she returned with three hotdogs wrapped in paper towels.

"Here you go, Cherokee braves. Take these back to eat with Little White Dove in your teepee."

While we were scarfing down the hotdogs I said again, "Now we have a teepee and food, just like real Indians."

But Britt still wasn't satisfied. "Well, I guess. But real Indians didn't eat hotdogs. They hunted buffalo."

"We don't have a buffalo," said Little White Dove.

"A cow," I reasoned, "is pretty much the same thing."

This time Little White Dove didn't argue. She just grabbed her papoose Libby and headed back to the house. We never saw her again, but we didn't care because that left Tall Man and Running Bear free to ride the western plains and hunt the Great White Buffalo, which actually was a red Hereford beef cow with a white face, but close enough.

Britt and I walked a short distance through the woods until we came to the pasture fence. Crawling beneath the strands of barbed wire, we stayed low until we spied our quarry grazing apart from the rest of the herd. With a blood curdling shriek, we jumped up to charge across the grassland, shooting rubber-tipped arrows. Our buffalo let out a bellowing moo and took off. Our pursuit was cut short by the crack of rifle fire. We froze in our tracks and did not move until we heard a voice call out, "Stop chasing the cow!" Turning around, we saw Britt's grandfather, who we called Poppy, standing at the end of his front porch holding a .22 rifle.

Britt yelled back, "That ain't no cow! That's our buffalo!"

Poppy pumped his rifle and said, "Stop chasing the buffalo then. You boys come here."

We ran across the pasture, crawled back under the barbed wire, and made our way up to Britt's grandparents' house. Poppy had returned to his seat on the opposite end of the long, shaded porch where he could look out over his cornfield. That's why he had the gun. He was shooting at crows threatening to destroy the crop, not boys chasing the cow. He just let us see the gun in his hand to make a point.

As we mounted the porch steps, Poppy took one look at us and said, "What you got your momma's Avon painted all over your face for?"

Britt answered, "I got a new book about Indians."

"You ain't no Indian," Poppy retorted. "Set down." We sat on the porch floor to watch Poppy take aim at a crow. *Pow!* Then he put the gun upright. "I'm gonna need you boys to fetch. Go get 'em."

We jumped off the end of the porch, ran out between the corn rows, found the dead crow, and brought it back to throw down in the grass. Then we sat back down on the porch floor and waited. Poppy took aim and fired again. *Pow!* We jumped up, but he said, "Wait, wait, wait. Safety first." After he shifted the rifle upright, he commanded, "Fetch!" And just like two faithful bird dogs, we retrieved another dead crow.

We played bird dogs for the better part of an hour until Poppy went into the house to lock his rifle in the gun cabinet. When he returned, he said, "You boys want to know something about Indians? I'll show you some real Indian stuff right here."

Stepping off the porch and walking to the edge of the field, he picked up a dried corncob laying on the ground next to one of the dead crows. Yanking three long black feathers from the crow's wing, he stuck them into the end of the corncob. Then he threw the cob into the air. We watched it float back down to the ground, the feathers twirling like the blades on a helicopter. Poppy looked at us and said, "That toy is called a whirligig. That's an Indian word."

I had never read that in *Childcraft* or *World Book Encyclopedia,* but as he had a .22 rifle with a scope, who was I to argue?

Then Poppy said, "I'll show you something else." He took out his pocketknife and chopped off the old dead crow's foot. Then he showed us how to pull at the frayed tendons hanging from the severed leg to make the toes on the foot curl up. We watched him perform this trick over and over until he said, "That there is an Indian yo-yo."

"Wow!" we exclaimed. "Where'd you learn that?"

Poppy said, "I didn't read it out'n no book!"

"What do you mean?" I asked.

"Well, I like Indians so good I went and married me one."

"You did?"

He looked at Britt. "Where's your grandma from?"

"Oklahoma."

"Did that book ever talk about 'The Trail of Tears?'"

"Yes sir, we know about that." The *Childcraft* book dedicated a whole chapter to the sad history of the Indian Removal Act and the forced migration of the Cherokee from the eastern woodlands to the plains of Oklahoma.

"Well, your grandma's great-grandma walked that trail."

We left our fake Indian junk laying on the porch and went charging into the house to find Britt's grandma in the kitchen.

"Granny, are you a Cherokee Indian?"

"I'm half," she informed us. "All the people on my mom's side were Western Band Cherokee from Oklahoma."

"Did your great-grandma walk The Trail of Tears?"

"Sure did. I never knew her, but I heard all the stories."

"Will you tell us?"

Granny looked all around the kitchen before she said, "Well, I would, but I have to peel these potatoes."

We grabbed potato peelers and went to work while Granny told us about her family. When she stopped talking, we begged for more. Glancing at a big bowl of green beans, she said, "I wish I could tell you more, but these beans need strung."

We got busy with the beans, and she kept going. Trading kitchen labor for stories, we spent the whole afternoon preparing dinner just to keep Granny talking. We didn't play Indians much after that because we had Granny. She was the real thing.

Besides, there were plenty of other historical topics in *World Book Encyclopedia*.

The riverbank just below the railroad tracks that ran behind my house was the perfect place to play World War II because of all the whiskey bottles. Back then, Harlan, Kentucky was a dry county; no liquor sales at all. But the neighboring county was wet, soaking wet. Bootleggers would truck illegal hooch into Harlan all the time. If you knew where to go, you could buy whatever you wanted from one of their places on the river. If rumors of a planned raid from the sheriff's office started to circulate, the bootleggers would pour out anything they couldn't drink in a hurry and throw the empty bottles into the water to let the current carry away any evidence of their illegal activity.

When Britt came to my house to play World War II, we would go down to the river to find Jack Daniels and Jim Beam bottles washed up on the bank. We plugged the bottles with handfuls of twisted grass, so when we tossed them back into the water, they would float. As the whiskey fleet traveled downstream, we would stand on the railroad tracks overlooking the river and throw rocks, pretending to be the Japanese bombing Pearl Harbor. With a good-sized railroad rock and decent aim, you could re-christen Jim Beam as the USS Arizona, sending the ship straight to its watery grave. We always felt a little bad about pretending to be the enemy bombing American ships, not to mention we were littering the river bottom with broken glass. So, we would pick a bunch of daisies and scatter them over the waves in a sort of wreath-laying ceremony.

One day we went down to the river to play Pear Harbor and discovered, much to our disappointment, the bootleggers had switched to cans of Bud Light. You just can't make a good USS Arizona out of a beer can. As we started back to the house by crossing over the railroad tracks, I discovered a treasure laying between the rails—an unopened can! I picked it up saying, "We read about this in *World Book*. You remember how World War II ended, right?"

Britt said, "We dropped the A-bomb."

I started shaking the can of beer as I said, "Look out, Hiroshima!" Then I started a countdown: "Ten, nine, eight, seven, six, five—"

"Wait, wait, wait!" Britt shouted. "Before they dropped the bomb, leaflets were scattered all over Japan warning civilians of the most destructive explosive ever known."

I handed Britt the can and said "Keep shaking!" as I snatched up a dandelion and blew all its little fuzzy seeds into the wind. "There! The leaflets have been distributed. Countdown resuming: Four, three, two, one!"

By now that Bud Light, warmed by the summer sun, had been shaken until the ends of the can were bulging out.

Britt yelled, "Bombs away!" as he tossed the can of beer high into the air. The explosion didn't produce a mushroom cloud, but we were covered in nuclear fallout. Being raised by teetotalers, we were afraid to go home covered in beer foam. We ended up riding our bikes to Britt's grandparents' house. By the time we arrived our clothes had dried. Thinking we were free of contamination, we joined Poppy on the front porch.

We realized our mistake when he took a big sniff and asked, "What's that smell?"

Britt said, "Nuclear fallout. We're World War II veterans."

"You ain't no veterans!" Poppy scoffed, then chuckled as he added, "Y'all smell like some of my buddies down at the VFW, but you ain't veterans."

"Do you know stuff about World War II?" I asked.

Poppy said, "I didn't read it out'n no book."

"You're a veteran?" asked Britt. "You fought in the war?"

"Fought in it? I won it."

We didn't answer.

Poppy stopped teasing and began to tell us about the war years. As I remember, it was one of the only times he ever really talked about it. He served as a ball turret gunner on a USAFF B-17 Flying Fortress conducting bombing runs over Nazi Germany. His plane was shot down, and he spent some time as a prisoner of war. When we asked about prison camp life he said, "Come in the house. I want to show you something."

We followed him into his bedroom, where he opened a footlocker that always sat at the end of his bed. Among the old photos and some patches he had saved from his uniform was a little flat box. He took the lid off to reveal a Purple Heart. When we inquired about some official looking papers folded up in the bottom of the box, he said, "That's documentation for a second Purple Heart, but I never sent it in."

We wanted to know why. Poppy stared at a photograph of several of his war buddies before answering. "A second medal, when others never got the chance to earn the first one, would just be selfish, wouldn't it?"

That was pretty much the end of playing World War II, but we continued to search *World Book Encyclopedia* for stuff to pretend. Britt and I agreed it was best to choose an event that happened so long ago there were no survivors to tell us we were doing it wrong. Being boys of the American South, of course we chose to reenact the Civil War.

✵✵✵

I had a miniature cannon that shot a real blast about as loud as Poppy's rifle. Britt had a soldier's kepi hat and a Confederate flag. With those props, we had everything we needed to fight The Battle of Gettysburg in my front yard. After a brief war council, it was decided Britt would man the cannon on the front porch and I would take up a position behind the goat shed about forty yards away. From there I could storm the porch yelling like a rebel and waving the Confederate flag. When Britt fired the cannon, I would take a dive into the grass. After performing this overly dramatic death scene, we would trade places and do it again.

It was a great plan, except for Britt's one concern: "Who's going to be General Grant?"

"I can't be General Grant. My people fought for the South."

"Well, I don't want to be General Grant either," argued Britt. "I want to shoot the cannon."

"General Grant can shoot the cannon if he wants to," I countered, but Britt wasn't convinced. We consulted the encyclopedia to learn if Ulysses S. Grant ever fired a cannon. But we never read the article because the first page of the entry displayed a picture of the distinguished gentleman in his dress uniform and full white beard, smoking a cigar. I realized my billy goat had a long white beard. All we needed was a cigar. We jumped onto our bicycles and rode about a half mile to a little country store. At first the storekeeper didn't want to sell a cigar to us, but when we explained it was for our goat, General Grant, he said okay.

We tied General "Billy Goat" Grant to a tree with a rope and stuck the stogie into his mouth. He stood there in the shade chomping on his cigar and looking stoic, just like his portrait in the encyclopedia. I put on the kepi hat and took the Confederate flag behind the goat shed to wait for Britt to set up the cannon on the porch. He was taking a long time, so I yelled, "Are you ready?"

He yelled back. "I'm ready if you're ready!"

"Are you sure you're ready? 'Cause I ain't gonna charge unless you're really ready!"

"I'm really ready!"

Believe it or not, that's pretty much how the Civil War went. Both sides lined up with everything they could get a hold of to kill each other, then started taunting "Are you ready?" Only thing was, we didn't think to ask our General Grant if he was ready.

I came charging out from behind the shed with a rebel yell just as Britt fired the cannon. *Bam!* We didn't realize General Grant was gun-shy. That goat reared up on his hind legs, pulling the rope with which he was tied as taut as a clothesline, effectively ending my realistic portrayal of

Pickett's Charge when it caught me right across my Adam's apple. My feet flew up even with my eyeballs, and I hit the ground so hard it knocked the wind out of my lungs. I was rolling around on the ground gasping for breath as Britt rolled around on the front porch laughing his head off. Not only was I horrified Britt would commit the mortal sin of laughing at the Confederate fallen, but I was in physical pain from a rope burn that started just under my left ear and went all the way across my throat to the right.

Britt apologized for making fun of my pain by saying, "Poppy will have some udder cream to rub on that."

We rode our bicycles down the road, past the country store and Britt's house to his grandparents' home, where we predictably found Poppy sitting on the front porch. After showing him my rope burn, he fetched a pot of udder cream from the milking barn and started applying it to my neck. I was still wearing the soldier's kepi hat. He grabbed the bill and yanked it down over my eyes as he said, "Well now, I've read that book. Tell me Johnny Reb, how'd you get this here red badge of courage?"

"We were playing Gettysburg."

"You ain't never been in no Civil War," Poppy snorted.

Britt looked at his grandfather, his eyes wide with shock. "How old are you?"

Poppy snapped the lid shut on the pot of udder cream and said, "Set down."

We really didn't want him to ruin another war for us, but we had been taught to respect our elders, so we sat down as he began his story. "Now 'round here, they weren't no big battles like Gettysburg, but up on Pine Mountain, there's that tall cliff what they call Rebel's Rock. During the war years there was a Billy Yank and a Johnny Reb that fought each other, but it had nothing to do with the North and South. They was fightin' over a woman and used the Civil War as an excuse to try and kill each other. Well, Billy Yank was chasin' his rival up the side of Pine Mountain and before Johnny Reb knowed what he was about, he come out on the top of that cliff. Now he was in a pickle, 'cause if he stayed there Billy Yank would shoot him, but if he jumped ..."

Poppy paused for dramatic effect. Britt and I didn't speak, we didn't move. Completely drawn into the story, we just waited until Poppy announced, "My teeth are loose." And without another word he got up and went into the house ... for nearly ten years.

We never heard the end of the story, because Granny called us into the kitchen to eat dinner. After that we watched *Wheel of Fortune.* Then we went back outside to catch lightning bugs until my mom called on the phone reminding me to ride my bike home before it got completely dark. The next day was Sunday, and my family went to church. Then it was Monday and a full week of school following. The next Saturday we played backyard baseball. The Saturday after that we went fishing. After school let out for the summer we went off to camp. Then there was middle school. Britt played football. I was in beginner band. Next came high school. We went to the beach on our senior trip. Britt chose a local college; I went out of state. Life is like that. Sometimes you never get to hear the rest of the story.

✵✵✵

When I went off to college, I was still trying to live my life "by the book," but as a theater major I had replaced *World Book Encyclopedia* with *The Collected Works of William Shakespeare.* I was cast as Octavius in the fall production of "Julius Caesar." It was thrilling to play a prominent role in a classic drama, but I had more than a little difficulty licking my southern accent. I gave it a valiant effort, but quickly realized interpreting British literature on the stage was not my forte. At the fall break, I returned home for the Thanksgiving holiday. My family joined Britt's family for a big turkey dinner at his grandparents' house. After the meal, I went outside to sit on the porch with Poppy.

After sitting a while just looking out over the cornfield and watching the sun set, Poppy spoke without turning to look at me. "Do you like school?"

"Yes, sir. I like it alright."

"You still set on studying that Shakespeare?"

"Yes, sir. I guess so."

"What do you mean 'you guess so'?"

"Well, I like it, but I'm not sure I'm cut out for it."

"I don't hold to that theater." He pronounced it like "thee-ay-ter" but I didn't say anything until he asked another question. "They got storytelling at your school?"

"Yes sir. As a matter of fact, theater majors get extra credit for taking a class in storytelling."

"I would do storytelling if'n I was you."

"I don't know what I'd talk about."

Poppy didn't answer right away, but eventually he said, "You could tell that story 'bout Rebel's Rock."

I snorted. "I never heard how it ended."

Poppy looked at me and said matter-of-factly, "Oh, he jumped."

Then he enjoyed watching as I struggled against the urge to shout "That's it?" He let the moment hang for so long I thought I would have to finish four years of college and earn a graduate degree before he spoke again. Finally, he continued. "Johnny Reb jumped into a great big hemlock tree growing alongside that tall cliff. Scrambling down the branches like a monkey on a ladder, he was able to run away and continue his fight with Billy Yank another day. As it turned out Billy Yank won the war, but Johnny Reb got the girl."

I laughed. Poppy just turned back to continue watching the sun slip down behind the mountain beyond his cornfield. After several minutes he asked, "Do you know how Johnny Reb knew there was a big hemlock tree next to that cliff for him to jump into?

"No, sir."

"He didn't read it out 'n no book."

I laughed again. "Well, where'd he learned it then?"

Poppy turned back towards me as he said, "I reckon his Poppy told him."

I didn't answer, and Poppy didn't say anything else. As we continued looking out over the cornfield, I didn't know what Poppy was thinking. I was sitting there working out how I could fit storytelling into next semester's class schedule. After the sun went below the mountain, the evening turned cool, what Poppy called "airish."

Standing up to leave, I broke the silence. "Well, it's getting cold and I better get on home. Are you going in the house?"

Poppy didn't answer, he just sat there. Knowing he had become more than a little hard of hearing, I spoke louder. "I'm leaving. Are you going inside?"

He still sat. Giving up, I walked to the end of the porch and started down the steps, but I stopped when I heard Poppy's chair creak. I turned back to discover him standing right behind me. He grabbed me and hugged me tight as he whispered in my ear, "I love you."

You won't read that in *World Book Encyclopedia*.

I AIN'T KNOW, BO

My very first introduction to the Gullah language came from Mr. Smoky and Mr. Stinky when I began working as a carriage-driving tour guide in the historic district of Charleston, South Carolina. I also had a mountaintop experience around the same time at St. John's Reformed Episcopal Church, where I learned how the language so beautifully and eloquently expresses the deeply meaningful religious life of African-American people in the Lowcountry. Both of those stories are in this book— "Smoky and Stinky" and "Stay on the Road." I suppose my third most memorable encounter with the Gullah language was somewhat a combination of the first two. It involved an ornery but lovable Gullah-speaking character, sort of a kid version of Smoky and Stinky, and it took place at a Christian school where religious life was freely and joyfully expressed on a regular basis.

After working as a tour guide, I taught eighth grade English for two years. (That's another story. See "Toilet Paper and a Troubled Teenager.") After that, I moved to Ferndale Baptist School in North Charleston, where I had twelve fifth graders in my classroom. I actually started the year with thirteen, but one of them was a bad egg. We prayed him right out of there. If you've ever taught school, you can guess how that went. He was sent off to some other school for about six weeks, where he turned another faculty to fervent prayer, and then he came back. Upon the bad egg's return, the principal left it up to me to decide if we should readmit him to our school.

We were a small, self-supporting institution with a shoestring budget, so I asked the principal, "How's the cash flow?"

He said, "We're flush. We don't really need the money."

I immediately made my decision. "Fine, don't let him back in. That takes my class down from a baker's dozen to an even twelve. Twelve was good enough for Jesus, twelve is good enough for me."

I had a lovely little group of disciples and I really enjoyed every day with them. Unlike my previous experience of teaching an eighth-grade class with a strong criminal element, I did not awake each morning with a stomachache. Instead, I was genuinely excited about the adventures I would have with my boys and girls. I would wake up thinking things like, *Oh yes, we're going to read a little play aloud today, and Joseph is an excellent reader. He will do well at that. And then we're going to start a fractions lesson. And Christine's very good at math. That'll be her moment to shine.* I had a great class, but it wasn't without its challenges.

I had a little boy named Mark. How to describe Mark? Well, he chose a seat in the back of the room. That was my first clue for potential trouble. Your "challenge" kids always choose to sit in the back. Knowing this, on the first day of school I allowed students to choose their own seat. Then on the following day I completely reversed the seating order so those who chose the back row were in the very front where I could keep an eye on them.

You know the poem about Santa Claus that says he shook when he laughed like a bowl full of jelly? That was Mark. When I had him seated in the front row and could study him closely, he reminded me more of a bowl of jelly than anything else. He was about as round as he was tall, and he just laughed and giggled, and wiggled and jiggled, through every lesson. He never took anything seriously. He did not pay attention. He did not follow along in his book. Everything was a joke. He was very much playing the role of the class clown. To be fair, I should note he was never disrespectful. He wasn't defiant or sassy or anything like that. No, he was a very respectful little boy, just a complete goofball.

In the very first week of the school year, we were reviewing what the students had learned the previous year in fourth grade. In English Language Arts, this included types of sentences.

I said, "All right, boys and girls, since this is just a quick review, I'm going to make it easy on you. I'm not going to make you write out a bunch of sample sentences. Let's just do this orally. I'll call out a type of sentence, and you raise your hand and give me an example. For instance, a declarative sentence. That's a sentence that makes a statement. Can somebody give me an example of a declarative sentence?"

My little star pupil, Christine, raised her hand and said, "I will go to school on Tuesday." She followed this simple statement by jabbing a finger in the air as if she were poking an imaginary target and simultaneously made a quick, raspberry sound with her mouth. "I will go to school on Tuesday—*pbbbt!*"

The poking finger and accompanying raspberry were very important. That's how I taught my students to note punctuation when dictating sentences. Years ago there was a comedian named Victor Borge who would do "oral punctuation." I showed my students a clip of his comedy routine and allowed them to do the same thing. (If you are not familiar with Victor Borge, YouTube him. He was a classic comedian and very inspirational to my students.) Whenever we dictated sentences or read aloud, the air was filled with sound effects: *Pbbbt! Boop! Click! Zip!* One of our favorites was the exclamation point, drawing our fingers down through mid-air, then ending with a jab and saying *"Yeeeow! Bam!"*

As the lesson progressed, I asked the class for an example of an interrogative sentence. Another one of my star pupils, a little boy named Joseph, raised his hand and said, "Will we go to school on Tuesday?" He simply turned the previous declarative sentence into a question. And of course he provided the proper sound effect for the punctuation as he drew a giant question mark in the air with his finger: *"Grrrrr! Boink!"*

I let the kids call out several more examples and the air was filled with sample sentences ending in *"pbbt, boop, click, zip,"* and so on. We were having a lot of fun. But I noticed Mark wasn't raising his hand. He had not learned what other kids already knew: If you don't know the answer, disguise yourself by raising your hand immediately because the teacher is going to pass over all the eager beavers to give the slower-to-respond kids a chance. He was just sitting there goofing off and not paying any attention.

Well, I am an equal opportunity educator. I said, "Mark, it's your turn. Can you give me an example of an imperative sentence, a sentence that gives a command?"

Whenever Mark was under pressure, when he didn't know the answer to a question or had been caught daydreaming, he would slip from English into his birth language, which was Gullah. Mark used lots of Gullah idioms and pronunciations in his speech. And on this occasion, he had no idea how to give an example of an imperative sentence, so he shrugged his shoulders and said, "Ah ain't know!"

I wanted to help him out and I sort of walked him toward a correct answer by saying, "An imperative sentence gives a command, it tells somebody to do something like 'Please, sit down.' or 'Don't touch that.' Can you give me another example?"

Mark just shrugged his shoulders again, added an eye roll, and said, "Ah ain't know, Bo!" which means, "I don't have a clue, brother!"

I tried again. "How about an easy one? Let's try a different type of sentence. How about an example of an exclamatory sentence? A sentence that you might shout. A sentence that shows great feeling. Can you give me an example of an exclamatory sentence?"

All of a sudden, his face lit up. He stood up from behind his desk and said, "I got this one!" He turned to face the class and proudly proclaimed "School sucks!" Then he drew an imaginary exclamation point in the air as he shouted an enthusiastic *"Yeeeow! Bam!"*

This example of an exclamatory sentence was loudly proclaimed in the fifth-grade classroom of a Baptist school. A very conservative Baptist school. Consequently, we had to take a trip to the principal's office. When we walked in I said, "Mark, tell the principal what you said."

He replied, "Ah ain't know, Bo!"

"No, no, no! Not the Gullah. Tell the principal what you said in English."

Now, lest you think that I never let my kids speak Gullah, that's not true. Oh no. We had a great love for the Gullah culture. We had lots of Gullah children who were the descendants of enslaved families in our school, and from time to time, we would have lessons featuring the Gullah language. We would read the New Testament in Gullah. Sometimes we prayed the Lord's Prayer in Gullah.

"*We Fada wa dey een heaben,*
*   leh everybody hona ya name.*
We pray dat soon ya gwine
*   rule oba all de wol.*
Wasoneba ting ya wahn,
*   leh um be so een dis wol sem like dey be dey een*
*   heaben.*
Gii we de food wa we need
*   dis day yah an ebry day.*
Fagib we fa duh bad ting we done do
*   Same like we da fagib dem people wa do bad ta we.*
Leh we dohn hab haad test wen Satan try we.
*   Keep we fom ebil.*
Yuh duh big boss mahn obah all ob we,
*   An we gib ya praise fuh ebeh and ebeh.*
A-mahn."

Finally, after a little prodding, Mark told the principal what he had shouted out in my class. "School sucks!"

The principal burst out laughing. "Mr. Lowry, you're new this year to our school. What you need to know is Mark has a brother in fourth grade named Marcus and he has a sister in third grade name Marqueesah. Then, there is a cousin in second grade named Marquee. And they're coming to you like stair steps, one after the other. So, you need to learn how to handle this and help Mark successfully progress from fifth grade to sixth grade, because we've learned through prior experience it's best not to have two family members in the same class." He patted Mark on the back, said, "Try to be a good boy, Mark," and sent him back to class!

I thought, *That's it? In Catholic school, they'd tie you up, or feed you only bread and water, or something!* How was I going to teach this boy when he wouldn't take anything seriously?

✱✱✱

My first opportunity to get Mark's attention came during our social studies time. We were studying world history and came across a chapter on ancient Egypt. My kids really got into it. They were fascinated with the pyramids, and the camels, and the sand, and all of that. We read about Hatshepsut, the only female pharaoh of ancient Egypt. We read she might have even been Moses' adopted mother from the Old Testament. It was all very interesting, and I tried to figure out how I could use it somehow or another to get Mark's attention. Inspiration struck the next morning when I was on my way to school.

It happened to be garbage pick-up day in my neighborhood, so everybody had their garbage bins pulled out to the curb. As I was driving along, I went past a garbage bin with two bare legs sticking out. I didn't even blink. This was North Charleston, murder capital of the world. But then I realized a murderer probably would have done a better job at stashing an actual body. I backed up and looked more carefully to discover the bare legs of a naked

Barbie doll that stood about three feet high. Some kid had taken a magic marker and drawn all over the doll, then used scissors to chop off most of its hair. The kid's mom had obviously considered the doll ruined and thrown it out. I grabbed the dead Barbie, tossed her into the back-seat of my car, and drove on to school.

As soon as class started, I gathered my children around and said, "Okay, boys and girls, you remember yesterday in our social studies book when we read about Hatshepsut, the only female pharaoh of ancient Egypt?" They nod-ded their heads. I continued in a dramatically lower voice, "She's in the back of my car." The kids gasped. "And when you see her, you'll see she died from some horrible skin disease. She isn't dressed properly for a royal burial so I thought maybe we could make her into a mummy." All the kids cheered.

Of course, I was thinking of Mark. What fifth-grade boy doesn't like dead people? Surely this would get his at-tention. We went out and got the doll from the back seat of my car and laid her out on my desk. With a big roll of duct tape from the custodian's closet we wrapped up our mummy. I shared information about how mummies were embalmed, how their organs were removed and stored in clay jars. It was a little weird and more than a little gross. The kids loved it!

After we had finished embalming Hatshepsut I said, "Now we've got other things we must study today, so I'm just going to set our mummy behind my desk. But tomorrow, ask your mom for a white bedsheet to bring to school. We'll dress up in our ceremonial robes and conduct an Egyptian funeral." I told them we would carry Hatshepsut's body overhead in a funeral procession down the hallway, clanging cymbals and falling prostrate before the Pharaoh. Then we would lay her in an empty classroom and turn it into a tomb by drawing hieroglyphics on the board with colored chalk. Everyone was very excited. Even Mark!

All my students returned the next morning draped in their white robes ... except for Mark. He was wearing a printed bedsheet with Star Wars figures all over it. Exasperated, I said, "Mark, Darth Vader was not an Egyptian!"

"Well, neither was Barbie!" he quipped.

So, we had our funeral with eleven white-robed Egyptians and Darth Vader. What was I going to do with this kid?

The next chapter in our social studies book was about ancient Greece and the Olympic Games. There were illustrations showing foot races, the discus throw, the javelin, and more. But what caught Mark's eye was an illustration of two men wrestling. Now, this was real wrestling, much like athletes in the modern Olympics, where they grapple for the strongest position on a matted gym floor. But Mark assumed this was the ancient origins of WWF, the

Worldwide Wrestling Federation. You know, Hulk Hogan and his crowd. I finally found the one thing Mark took seriously and was *very* passionate about. After that social studies lesson, every sample sentence, every oral presentation was about WWF. His favorite wrestler was Junkyard Dog, and he could tell you every statistic about the man. Mark was constantly using wrestling lingo. He peppered his speech with terms like "pile driving" and "body slamming" and "top rope." In fact, that was the way Mark gave you a compliment.

One day I wore a bowtie Mark particularly liked and he said, "That bowtie is top rope, dude!"

By this time I had learned to just go with it. So I responded, "Thanks, Junkyard Dog."

And he barked at me.

If Mark finished his seat work early, he would go to the art supply shelf and grab a big, long piece of black construction paper and some golden yellow paper. Using scissors he would cut an oval shape out of the golden yellow paper and staple it to the middle of the big long black strip to fashion himself a wrestling belt. He was forever getting into trouble for pile driving his friend James into the sandbox on the playground.

I would tell him, "Mark, we do not have contact sports at this school. We are Baptists. We only lay hands on another if we're about to dunk them underwater. Leave James alone!"

I didn't know what to do.

☆☆☆

Fifth grade—and by "fifth grade" I mean mostly Mark—presented daily challenges. So, for a change of pace I volunteered to teach English as a second language to adults at the public library. This was kind of a little service project from our church and school. The free class met on Sunday afternoons in the library conference room. I mistakenly assumed I would have a handful of Hispanic people and maybe one or two students from an Asian country. As it turned out, I had twelve Russian senior citizens. My youngest student was sixty-nine years old and my oldest student was eighty-five.

They sat down at our first meeting and said, "We want you to for help us. Please, help us for to learn English language of our new home in United States."

I could tell they had practiced this sentence and had done their best to prepare for their first lesson. With their nervous attempt to speak English I was completely hooked. *At last!* I thought, *earnest students who will take their studies seriously!*

I thought wrong.

For ESL (English as a Second Language) lessons, we had a curriculum called *Word by Word.* I would lay out a big book across the conference table with a picture page of life in these United States. Then I would lead the class in a discussion of what we saw in the illustration. It might be a picture of the interior of a grocery store, and we would practice how to go shopping. I would teach them phrases like "Does that include the tax?" and "Where can I find the milk?" I would help them practice how to respond when the bagger asked, "Paper or plastic?" That kind of thing. Survival English for immigrants.

Bless their hearts! My Russian students worked so hard on their lessons, laboring over anything I assigned to them. They would try to compose essays by writing several paragraphs in their native language then looking up every word in a Russian/English dictionary and laboriously copying each word over into their new language. I say that my students worked very hard. That's mostly true, but there was Avraam Mikulinskiy. Avraam was like the Russian version of Mark. He was shaped like a bowl full of jelly and to him everything was a joke.

One day our lesson was on the topic of favorite foods. To give my students practical experience in conversational English, I went around the table and asked each one of them to name their favorite food and tell me how to make it. As I worked my way from student to student I came to Ganna, Avraam's wife. Ganna was a very conscientious student. She was well prepared for my question.

"Ganna, what is your favorite food?"

She replied in the tone of someone who had worked hard to memorize a speech. "Mr. Lorry." (All of my Russian students called me Mr. "Lorry," because try as they might they simply could not say "Lowry.") "Mr. Lorry, I enjoy eating hamburger. For to make a hamburger one must accumulate beef, lettuce, tomato, and bread known in grocery store as a bun . . ." Ganna had worked very hard with her Russian/English dictionary to prepare a whole essay on how to make a hamburger.

Then it was Avraam's turn. And I thought, *Now this is Avraam's chance to shine,* because he only knew one sentence in English. "I like ice cream." This was Avraam's answer to everything. You could ask, "What time is it?" "I like ice cream." "Do you have grandchildren?" "I like ice cream." "Who will you vote for in the next presidential election?" "I like ice cream." Like Mark, Avraam had his own way of saying he had no idea what you were talking about. His pet phrase "I like ice cream" served as the Russian equivalent to the Gullah expression, "Ah ain't know, Bo!"

I began. "Avraam, I have a question for you? Are you ready? You're going to like this one. Avraam, what is your favorite food?"

He smiled broadly. "I like ice cream."

"Very good! Can you tell us—in English—how to make ice cream?"

Long silence.

Then he said, "For making ice cream. You take wife. You put wife in freezer and you say, 'Wife, you no come out until ice cream!'"

All the other class members snickered and Avraam laughed out loud at his joke, his big belly bouncing up and down as he chuckled.

I laughed, too. Without thinking I said, "Ha, ha, very funny. There is a fifth-grade student I want you to meet. His name is Mark." Suddenly I realized I had hit on an idea! *I know what I'm going to do. I'm going to pair my fifth graders at Ferndale Baptist School with my Russian students as penpals and let them help each other out.*

At the end of each week, the kids had already gone to all of their special area classes. They'd done music, they'd done PE, they'd been to art, and we had about a half hour on Friday afternoons where we needed something to fill the time. I went to the bookstore and bought a *Teach Yourself Russian* book and cassette tape and did what poor schoolteachers do everywhere—I photocopied that book twelve times over and handed out pages to each fifth grader! We would listen to the Russian language tape and practice. We were learning Russian for tourists. "Where is the restroom?" "Do you have a restroom?" "Must one be a member of the Communist Party to use the restroom?" Stuff like that. We also learned how to greet people with "Dobroe utro!" (good morning), "Dobroe den!" (good day), and "Dobroe vecher" (good evening). My kids very much enjoyed learning a foreign language. They called our language study on Friday afternoons their "Russian Club."

After a while I announced to the Russian Club that each fifth grader was going to get a babushka or dedushka—a Russian grandmother or grandfather—to whom they could write letters. My kids loved this assignment.

They intuitively understood their penpal was learning to speak English and that reading letters from a fifth grader was practical experience for them. My kids labored over their letters just like my Russian students labored over their essays, working hard to craft excellent examples in spelling and grammar. I would pair them up to proofread each others' compositions and I'd hear things like:

"You forgot to capitalize that sentence."

"It don't matter. You know what I mean."

"No, it's not for me. It's for our Russians!"

They would always refer to them as "our" Russians. Like they were collecting baseball cards or something. These are my Russians and those are your Russians. I'll trade you a Lenin for a Trotsky!

I played mailman, delivering letters back and forth between the two groups. As you can imagine, the Russian grandmas and grandpas labored over each letter they wrote to their fifth-grade penpals with equal determination in getting the words just right. I had Mark write to Avraam. I figured that despite the language barrier, they would still understand each other.

Whenever I delivered a letter from Mark to Avraam, Avraam would smile, look at the envelope and say, "This letter from good boy Mark, yes?" Then he would immediately pass the letter to his wife Ganna to read and translate for him. Of course, every letter was about the Worldwide Wrestling Federation.

One day Ganna stopped reading and with a very confused look on her face asked, "Mr. Lorry, what this body slam? I no understand this."

I tried to explain. "Well, Mark is using wrestling lingo."

"Lingo?"

"He is speaking with lots of idioms. Do you know what those are?"

Ganna answered with exasperation. "Ah, idiom is very hard. Very difficult. I try for to learn this, but it impossible. In America everyone use idiom. People say 'It rain cat and dog.' I no see dog fall from sky! This very, very difficult!"

I explained idioms were common in every language and assured her that if I were to visit Russia I would encounter idioms that made no sense to me. I tried to help her not feel so frustrated. Then I said, "While we are on the subject, as your ESL teacher I should also talk to you about slang."

"What is slang?"

"Well, perhaps we will have a whole lesson on slang one day, but for now it is enough to know there are some things people say that are not nice words, bad words. Do you understand?"

Ganna quickly uttered the phrase all my Russian students said when they understood. "Ah, dah, dah, dah! (Oh, yes, yes, yes!) Then she continued, "I learn this in my study of English vocabulary. Some words must not be spoken as they are," she paused, struggling with the pronunciation, "in-ap-pro-pri-ate!"

Nodding, I went a step further. "For instance, even if you find learning something new to be difficult, you should not say "School sucks!"

"What this mean? School suck? It inappropriate?"

"Yes, it is inappropriate."

Ganna nodded. "Thank you, Mr. Lorry. You are good teacher. English language is very difficult, but I will no say 'suck.'"

✵✵✵

After several weeks of exchanging letters I decided we should go on a field trip together so everyone could meet his or her penpal in person. Both groups were anticipating the big day with much excitement, particularly my fifth graders, who had been practicing their Russian vocabulary for about eight weeks. We had not told our penpals we were studying the Russian language. It was going to be a surprise!

On the big day, all of my kids piled onto the school bus and we rode off to the retirement home where "our" Russians lived. When the bus pulled into the circular drive, Michael Cogan, a tall, thin, distinguished looking Russian man with wispy white hair was waiting for us. As soon as the bus came to a stop he climbed aboard, mounting the big steps slowly but surely. Then he looked at my students and said, "Zdravstvuite! Ya Mikaela." He was going to translate what he had just said to English. "Hello, My name is ..."

But before he could finish, my kids returned his formal greeting with their own. "Zdravstvuite! Dedushka Mikaela! Dobroe utro!"

Michael turned to look at me with big tears welling up in his eyes. "Mr. Lorry, your children are very beautiful. They greet me with Russian language. Hello, Grandfather Mikaela, Good morning! This is very nice. These beautiful children remind me of my baby time—No, how for to say this?"

"Your childhood."

"Ah, dah, dah, dah! These beautiful children remind me of my childhood when I was young boy in old country. Your children very smart, very good, very beautiful."

I began to realize this experience was very meaningful to "our" Russians. They loved their new country and were proud to be naturalized citizens, but they missed familiar customs and traditions. I began to pray, *Oh, please Lord, let them understand whatever he says next.* Our Russian was so very elementary. I didn't want Michael to be disappointed if he launched into a long speech and the kids had no idea what he was saying. Michael gestured to the long, front porch of the retirement home and the many rocking chairs sitting there. He looked at my children and said, "Sadit'sya, pozhaluysta."

My fifth graders nearly exploded with excitement. They had just experienced the thrill of hearing a foreign language and realizing their study and practice was paying off. They understood completely. Turning to me and all shouting at once they exclaimed, "He said, 'Sit down!' He said, 'Sit down, please!'"

"Very good," I said. "You may get off the bus and take a rocking chair. And make sure you say thank you to Mr. Michael for his kindness."

My kids started to file off the bus and in a chorus they chimed, "Thank you."

"No, no," I corrected. "In Russian. You know how to say thank you in Mr. Michael's language."

They all chorused "Spasibo!"

And Michael responded with "Spasibo tebeh!" (No, thank you!)

My kids did not understand Michael was praising them for saying it in Russian. They thought he was correcting their pronunciation. So they tried again. "Spasibo!" And Michael tried again "Spasibo tebeh!" My kids repeated, only louder, "Spasibo!" And Michael reciprocated "SPASIBO TEBEH!" Mercifully, this exchange, which was degenerating into a complete miscommunication, was interrupted by the arrival of the rest of our Russian friends. There were introductions all around, handshakes, hugs, and even some formal bowing. Finally, we all boarded the school bus for our field trip.

Once we were underway, I tried to redeem myself and my students from the little "Thank you and thank you" exchange by having them demonstrate their knowledge of the Russian language for their penpals. I said, "Boys and girls, let's show our Russian friends how we order lunch." I required my kids to order their lunch at the school cafeteria in Russian, so they knew lots of vocabulary words for foods. Their favorite food, of course, was hot dogs. I said, "Tell them how you would order a hot dog in Russian."

My kids beamed with pride and said, "Dah, Mr. Lowry. Goryachiy sobaka!"

Our Russians burst out laughing.

I said, "What? What's wrong?"

"Your children no say hot dog. They say 'dog on fire!'"

The fifth graders burst out laughing. Very quickly the whole group was engaged in a little lesson in how to properly say "hot dog" in the Russian language, which translates roughly to "sausage sandwich."

It wasn't long before we arrived at the Charleston Museum. Now, why did we go to the Charleston Museum? Because they have an Egyptian mummy. We were going to look at a real dead person! Very exciting! I had previewed the museum, making a list of twenty different objects to create a scavenger hunt of sorts. I had written the list twice in two columns, once in English and again in Russian. Then I had jumbled the lists. My fifth graders were to walk through the museum with their penpal, find the objects, and match them up, teaching each other the vocabulary words. We didn't know the Russian word for mummy, but we knew the Russian word for dead, which is "kaput." So you could match "dead" to "kaput" when you found the four-thousand-year-old sarcophagus.

I sent everybody off on the scavenger hunt. Of course, Mark was paired with Avraam Mikulinskiy. I sent Avraam's wife along with them to make sure Mr. "Ah Ain't Know Bo" and Mr. "I Like Ice Cream" didn't get into any trouble.

About forty-five minutes later Avraam, Ganna, and Mark returned from their walk around the museum. Ganna had taken a real shine to Mark. She had her arm around him, pinching his cheek, hugging him up. Avraam was walking along behind smiling and nodding.

Ganna turned to me with a big smile and said, "Mr. Lorry, Mark is good student. Yes?"

I shook my head, "Nyet. I am sorry to say that Mark is not a good student." I explained to her that Mark was a merry fellow and very likable, but he goofed off in class.

Ganna needed a little clarification. "What this mean, goof off?"

"Well, you remember our conversation about slang? Mark is the one who says, 'School sucks.'"

Suddenly, Ganna Mikulinskiy turned back to face Mark and her husband standing close behind him. There was fire in her eyes. I had no idea she was a retired schoolmaster. *From Russia!* First she addressed her husband Avraam. "Sadit'sya! You, sit down!"

With a sheepish look on his face he sank onto a bench and said, "I like ice cream."

Then she grabbed Mark by the ears and spun his head around so that he was facing her directly and just unloaded on him! "Marcus, you must study. You must work hard. Mr. Lorry, nice man. He has good method. He work hard for you. He love you. He love Russia. He love America. He love student. You no say 'suck' to Mr. Lorry! Mr. Lorry is good man. Mr. Lorry is teacher *from God!*"

For months after this little episode, I could always snap Mark back to attention by asking him, "Mark, who am I?"

"I know, I know. You're the teacher from God."

Ganna continued. "In Russia there is no opportunity. Many children, no education. It very hard. In America, much opportunity. Everyone happy. Everyone happy, happy in America. It like Disney World. In Russia it not happy. People say 'How are you?' People not happy, they say 'Oh, my back, my head, the KGB!'"

In her way, Ganna was trying to help Mark value his education, but she could see there was a communication barrier. He was looking at her and listening to her speech intently, but not really understanding what she was getting at. He just enjoyed the attention and stood there grinning from ear to ear.

Desperate to make him understand, Ganna, still holding him by the ears walked Mark across the museum lobby to a display board with information about slavery in the South Carolina Lowcountry. She pointed to an illustration of people in chains and practically shouted, "Marcus! No education is like slavery!"

Mark immediately went completely sober.

After a few seconds, he turned around and looked at me. "Could I have another paper?"

"Sure."

"Can we go through the museum again?"

"Yes."

They went off through the museum again. Mark and Ganna with their heads together, Avraam shuffling along behind, the three of them whispering things, laughing, exchanging words, working on their assignment. It was like Gullah meets Gorbachev! A cultural exchange that would have made the United Nations envious!

The next day I had my kids write thank you notes to our Russians for accompanying us on our field trip. Mark sat down and started furiously scribbling on a piece of paper. I reminded him, "Mark, don't rush. Do your best work." But he finished in a flash, put the note into an envelope, sealed it, and gave it to me to deliver to his penpals. Having finished so quickly, he had extra time while the other boys and girls were still writing. He went to the art shelf and took out a long strip of construction paper and started making himself a wrestling belt.

"I told you not to do that," I fussed at him.

He put up a hand. "You're going to like this, Mr. Lowry. You're going to like this!"

"I don't believe you, but I'm going to give you the benefit of the doubt. We'll see."

Later that day at recess I found Mark with his friend James on the playground. They were standing on either side of the sandbox. Both were wearing homemade wrestling belts. All of a sudden Mark jumps into the sandbox and yells, "Zdravstvuite!" Then James jumps into the sandbox from the opposite side and yells back, "Hello!" Then they both growl like two wild animals.

"What are you two doing?" I asked.

Mark explained. "This is my new game, Mr. Lowry. I call it 'Russian Challenge.' I jump into the sandbox and I say something in Russian, then James has to jump in from the other side and translate. If he gets it wrong. I take his wrestling belt. Then it's his turn and if I get it wrong, he takes my wrestling belt."

I was very impressed. "I like it! You go, Junkyard Dog!"

"No, no!" Mark said. "That's my old name. I have a new wrestling name—GORYACHIY SOBAKA! DOG ON FIRE!"

✡✡✡

When I delivered the thank you notes I was dying to see what Mark had written to the Mikulinskiys. Ganna was happy to show me the letter.

> Dear Ganna and Avraam,
> Thank you for going on the field trip with me. Thank you for helping me.

I WILL NOT BE A SLAVE.
Love,
Mark

That was it. The whole note was just three sentences, with the final statement written in all caps. Since the rest of the page was blank, Mark had filled in the empty page by writing with a big, fat magic marker:

Ganna, YOU IS DUH BOMB!

I asked, "Ganna, do you understand what that means?
"I no understand. What this mean 'You is duh bomb?"
Before I could answer, Avraam, Mr. I Like Ice Cream, leaned back in his chair, folded his arms over his big stomach, and grinning widely with a mischievous look on his face said, "Ah ain't know, Bo! It's American idiom!"

TOILET PAPER AND
A TROUBLED TEENAGER

I went to Belk's department store to buy a pair of new school shoes. New schoolteacher shoes. I asked the salesclerk if there might be a discount for educators.

She asked me, "What grade do you teach?"

I replied enthusiastically, "Eighth grade, my first year!"

She shook her head. "We don't have an educator's discount, but I'll give you twenty percent off for baptism by fire."

The sales lady must have been a prophet, because her biblical reference proved to be spot-on.

I could write a book filled with chapters about each one of my students, but I will limit myself to one story about a particular kid who sat in the back row of my second-period class. To protect his identity, I'll call him "Hood," which is a reference to his signature wardrobe. He wore a quilted parka every single day, even in August when the temperature was ninety-five degrees in the shade. The drab olive coat was always zipped up to the chin and the fur-trimmed hood was always flipped up over the student's head. In this heavy-duty survival sportswear, Hood set up camp in the very back of my classroom and did absolutely nothing. Like the proverbial "old man of the mountain," he never spoke, never raised his hand, never made an audible sound.

By the end of the first grading period, he was failing everything. Consequently, a parent-teacher conference was called. Now, a parent-teacher conference in elementary school is a simple affair. There's the parent and the teacher, and they confer. But eighth grade is middle school. The student has a team of teachers and they gang up on the parent. When we asked his mother to come in for a chat, there was a whole phalanx of educators arrayed on one side of a conference table and Hood's mother sitting all alone on the other. A guidance counselor sat at the head of the table. Seated next to her was the PE teacher, then the science teacher, then the social studies teacher, then the math teacher, and finally me, the English Language Arts teacher.

It was like a firing squad.

"He won't do this."

"He didn't turn in that."

"Doesn't pay attention."

"He sleeps in class."

"Refuses to try."

"Unwilling to engage."

Boom, boom, boom, right down the line. After each teacher had taken their shot, the guidance counselor, who was facilitating the meeting asked, "Mrs. Hood, is there anything you'd like to say?"

The mother just sat there in silence. Finally, the guidance counselor reached out with an open hand and simply said, "It's okay."

Words began to flow, along with plenty of tears. It was awful. I grew up in a very happy and stable home, so I had no experience with the type of situation she described. I'm sure even though she had been in the direct line of fire, I was the one who looked shell-shocked.

The mother spoke for several minutes and provided plenty of detail, but to summarize she basically said, "My husband and I have had problems for years. This past summer, just before school started, he left without warning. We have not heard from him in weeks. We really don't expect to hear from him ever again. My son is devastated. He has tried to commit suicide—twice."

When she stopped talking, several teachers immediately apologized for being insensitive and the guidance counselor assured her none of us knew about these awful circumstances. I didn't say anything, not even "I'm sorry." I didn't know what to say. The conversation continued around me. I was truly dumbstruck. If someone else spoke, if the guidance counselor asked the question, "What do you need?" I didn't hear it.

Apparently, the mother had said, "I think what my son needs is a male role model."

Well, the female guidance counselor glanced at the female PE teacher, who looked at the female science teacher, who turned to the female social studies teacher, who peered at the female math teacher, and finally all eyes were on me.

I said, "Perhaps he would benefit from some tutoring."

As the words escaped my lips I could feel my face turning red with embarrassment. How stupid! The boy's dad deserted him, he was flunking every subject, his mom was distraught because her son was suicidal and my feeble suggestion was he get some help with his homework? I wanted to die. Now it was the guidance counselor and my fellow teachers' turn to be stunned into silence. I'm sure they were sitting there thinking, "Wow, so this is what college is turning out these days."

But they didn't have time to say anything, because Mrs. Hood grabbed my hand, shook it enthusiastically, and said, "That would be great. Thank you for volunteering. I don't get off work until five o'clock. Since school lets out at three thirty, that means he can come to your room every day after classes for ninety minutes, then I'll be here to pick him up."

Before I could respond, she was gone; the meeting was over. The rest of the day passed in a blur. At three thirty that afternoon I found myself sitting behind my desk staring at Hood, who was seated in his accustomed place along the back wall, with a whole empty classroom between us. I had no idea what to do. I was only sure of one thing. I was a newly minted teacher about to give it the old college try!

"Hood, we had a very positive conversation with your mom this morning."

I was lying my pants off. It was the most horrible parent-teacher conference I could imagine, but I couldn't tell him that. I didn't know much, but I knew that he didn't need to hear that!

I continued. "She thinks it would be a good idea—and I agree—for you to come here every afternoon for tutoring. We'll start with English. After we get that in hand we'll move on to math and social studies and science. I can't promise, but if we work hard maybe by Christmas your report card will look better. What do you think?"

He turned sideways in his chair, so all I could see was the profile of his big parka and the fur-lined hood. Resistance. I knew about this. It's called "a reluctant learner," and I knew what to do for a reluctant learner. My teacher college training was proving useful after all. The technique is called "monitor and adjust."

So I changed tack by saying, "Well, maybe that's too much pressure. How about this? Your mom is not coming to pick you up until five o'clock every afternoon and you can't be wandering around the school unsupervised. You're stuck with me. But that might not be so bad, because you can use my room for a study hall, a nice quiet place to get your homework done."

I waited. No response. I kept going. "I won't bother you. You don't need to bother me. I'll just sit up here and do teacher stuff. You can sit back there and do your homework. We won't get in each other's way. And with all your homework done every afternoon, you'll never have to take a book home. What do you think?"

He turned all the way around in his chair so all I could see was his back. And just like that, I was out of techniques from teacher college. They don't tell you what to do when a student turns his back. Consequently, I resorted to what every educator does when his teacher college training utterly fails him.

I started yelling. "Well fine, just fine. I tried to help you, but you won't even meet me halfway. Which is a literal statement, because here I sit at the front of this classroom and you all the way in the back with all these empty chairs between us! Here's what's going to happen. You are going to get a piece of paper and a pencil. You are going to write down all your homework assignments. Then I'm going to write next to each one of them refused, refused, refused, so your mother will have documentation that I at least tried to help you!"

Hood unzipped his book bag. Refusing to look at me, he slowly pulled out a piece of paper. Then he slowly fished around in the book bag until he came up with a pencil. It was broken. He took his time finding another pencil.

At last I said in a quieter but still exasperated tone, "Now, let's start with my class. What is your homework assignment for English Language Arts?"

He didn't speak. I held my ground. Finally, he begrudgingly answered my question. "We are supposed to write a process."

It was a simple writing lesson. The teacher's manual had listed all kinds of possible topics: how to bake a cake, how to fold a paper airplane, how to do jumping jacks. The topic didn't really matter as long as the students demonstrated they could write clear, step-by-step instructions. Of course, the trick was to get eighth graders interested enough, motivated enough, to complete the assignment. The curriculum guide tried to be relevant by suggesting kids at this age are looking forward to getting a driver's license, and they could write driving directions from the school to their home. "First, make a left turn out of the school parking lot. After driving approximately three-quarters of a mile, turn right onto Oak Avenue, etc."

It also suggested that the teacher write driving directions from the school to their own home to show the students as an example. Well, I might have been a greenhorn teacher, but I wasn't a complete idiot. I had a significant criminal element in my class. There was no way I was going to make burglary easier for them by providing directions to my house. (You might think accusing fourteen-year-olds of serious crime is a bit of an overstatement. Let me remind you that I began this story by saying I could write a book about teaching eighth grade. Someday I probably will, but I must wait until the statute of limitations runs out.)

I ditched the curriculum guide and went with something different. No driving directions that would facilitate midnight theft, but something that was equally appealing when it came to deviant behavior. I suggested the kids write short essays detailing how to play a practical joke or how to pull off their favorite prank. It was almost Halloween and I thought a joke or a prank would be a lot more fun than anything suggested in the teacher's manual.

During class I told them about all kinds of practical jokes I had played when I was a teenager. When the subject of toilet paper came up, I told them TPing somebody's house was for amateurs. One time my friends and I ditched a church youth group Halloween party and toilet-papered a man's horse!

So that afternoon, when Hood said the homework assignment was to write a process, I asked him, "Can you do that? Can you write down a paragraph or two telling me how to play a joke on somebody?"

"No."

I prodded a little deeper. "Have you ever pulled a prank with some of your friends?"

"No."

I didn't pry any further, because a voice deep down in my heart said, "Tim, he's telling you the truth." I realized this boy probably had never played a joke, because you have to be brave to do such a thing. This kid was afraid; so afraid that he had tried to escape his own existence by attempting suicide. Twice.

The voice said again, "He's telling you the truth."

I recognized that voice. It was the Holy Spirit. I breathed a silent prayer in response. "What do I do?"

And the Holy Spirit said, "Just follow my lead."

I heard myself say, "Toilet paper! We talked about that in class today. If you could toilet paper any classroom in this school, which one would you pick?" I didn't know Hood had failed a science test earlier that day.

He answered without hesitation. "I'd toilet paper the science lab."

Next thing I knew, I felt myself rise up out of my chair and walk across the room. I turned in the doorway, looked back at Hood, and said, "If you think you're man enough, come on."

What was I doing? This was my very first teaching assignment. I had been on the job six whole weeks. It was like I was outside my body watching myself do something stupid! But I saw a glint of light in Hood's eye. Besides, I was following the Holy Spirit, and now Hood was following me. As we were walking down the hall I thought to myself, *No, no, no! This is not going to happen. There has to be a way out of this.* And then I remembered a bible verse from my childhood Sunday School days. "The Lord will not suffer you to be tempted beyond that which you are able to bear, but with the temptation will also make a way of escape."

I knew the way of escape. The custodian's closet where the toilet paper was stored would be locked. I was certain. Have you ever taught in public school? Supply is limited; they guard toilet paper as if the stuff was solid gold. I have actually heard a school principal remind the faculty that you could stretch your allotment by separating the plies.

It's ridiculous. Because of the scarcity, I figured the custodian's closet would not only be locked but subject to constant surveillance.

Nope! The door was wide open and not a single person was in the hall to witness what we were about to do. We snatched three rolls the size of truck tires, like they have in the dispensers in a Walmart restroom.

As we carried them down the hall I thought, *There's still a way out of this. The science lab will be locked. There are computers in there and all kinds of expensive equipment. There's no way we'll be able to get into that room.*

Nope! Like the miracle of the custodian's closet, this door was also standing wide open. The path before me was clear, so I led the way. For the next thirty to forty-five minutes, we busied ourselves using up all three of those industrial-sized rolls of toilet paper. We wrapped everything in the room. We filled every drawer of the filing cabinet with toilet paper. We climbed up onto the lab tables to reach the ceiling where we festooned the place with streamers of toilet paper hanging down everywhere. It looked like the Senior Prom of the Apocalypse. When we finally finished, we stood atop one of those lab tables, looked upon our work, and saw that it was good. As we walked out of the classroom, Hood slammed the door shut and I heard the lock click. There was no way to go back and undo what I had just done. So, I decided I might as well go help a troubled teenager write his first (and possibly last) essay. We ran down the hall back to my classroom.

"How about now?" I asked. "Could you write me a short essay, detailing the steps for toilet-papering a science lab?"

Hood didn't answer, but he enthusiastically grabbed the pencil he had left on his desk and started writing on the piece of blank notebook paper. I had never seen him write before. Except for our recent toilet paper escapade, I had never seen him do anything before. As he wrote, I noticed he was left-handed. He was holding his pencil in that awkward way of left-handed writers, with his arm crooked over the top of his paper. I almost asked, "Why don't you try to write with your right hand?" I know it was God Himself who kept my mouth shut.

After all the activity in the science lab, Hood was overly warm in his big parka. He stopped writing just long enough to put down his pencil, unzip the coat, and shrug it off to the floor. That was the first time I had really noticed his right hand. It had always been hidden inside the coat. Even when we were tossing toilet paper around the science lab I hadn't noticed. Now, I could clearly see his right hand was misshapen. He had no fingers. Just four little stumps and a regular thumb. It was clear why he always hid it away inside that coat. The handicap, though minor as handicaps go, was just one more thing. He didn't need one more thing.

When Hood finished writing, I asked if I could read his essay. The penmanship was atrocious, but I managed to decipher it. I marked an "A" at the top of the page.

"That was just fine. And that's not a sympathy grade because you're so far behind. I don't give sympathy grades. You earned it."

He didn't say anything as he put the paper and pencil into his backpack.

At that moment his mother walked into the room. She looked at her son and asked, "What'd you do with Mr. Lowry?"

"Nothing."

I chose not to elaborate. I knew we had a pact. I just smiled and said, "We made a little progress today and I'm very anxious to work with him again tomorrow."

Hood and his mom left and I went home. Not to write an essay, but to compose my last will and testament because I figured the punishment for toilet papering a science lab was probably death.

The next morning as I was getting ready to go to my execution—I mean school—I decided it might be a good idea to engage in some damage control by giving the science teacher a little warning. Before walking out the door, I grabbed the phone. She answered on the first ring.

"Debbie! I'm so glad I caught you before you left for school." She asked me why I was calling. "I just want you to know that when you get to school, you are going to find a surprise in your science lab. It's a bit unusual, but I know all about it and can explain when I get there."

Debbie was constantly collecting specimens for her science students, and she sounded excited when she asked, "Oh, did you find me an interesting bug?"

"No, it's not a bug. You'll see." I hung up the phone, confident she wouldn't freak out and under the false impression I had covered all the bases. However, I had not taken into account that science teachers don't unlock school buildings first thing in the morning. Assistant principals do.

Our assistant principal was named Mr. Barnes and he was only half human. The rest of him was pit bull. Every student in the school was scared of Mr. Barnes. When he walked through the hallways, all he had to do was simply look at a kid and they would immediately say, "I didn't do it. I swear. I don't know what it is, but whatever it is, I didn't do it." He could snap a finger and boys would start emptying their pockets to show they weren't carrying any contraband. Even the teachers feared Mr. Barnes. Admittedly, we needed him to be scary, because of the significant criminal element in our school. As a teacher I appreciated his no-nonsense approach to discipline, until the morning after I had become a member of that criminal element.

I was standing behind my desk checking attendance when I heard a low growl. I looked up to see Mr. Barnes standing in my door. "Mr. Lowry, I have a situation and I need to speak to you out here in the hallway."

I immediately realized I had telephoned the wrong person earlier that morning. I glanced back at my students and in that moment decided it was best for me not to join Mr. Barnes in the hallway, but to hang with my gang instead. We delinquents needed to stick together. (That's not an exaggeration. I had one girl who attended morning classes by special permission from her parole officer. She came to English Language Arts in her orange jumpsuit.) I was staying with my posse.

I looked back at the assistant principal and said, "Mr. Barnes, you are very familiar with several of these students. I cannot leave them unsupervised. Why don't you just step into my classroom and whisper into my ear."

He crossed the room and strode up to my desk. There was no whispering. "Mr. Lowry, somebody broke into this school last night and toilet-papered the science lab!"

I glanced to the back of the room. There was Hood in his regular seat. He was wearing his trademark parka coat. As I caught his eye, he flipped the hood up and started shaking his head back and forth. We had a pact; I couldn't rat him out. So, I took a deep breath and turned back to Mr. Barnes with feigned surprise. "No!"

The entire room fell silent. All eyes were on me and the assistant principal. He began an interrogation. "Mr. Lowry, did you call the science teacher and say you had a surprise for her?"

"Yes, as a matter of fact, I did."

"I need you to tell me the surprise."

I looked at Hood. Hood looked at me. "Well, if I told you, it wouldn't be a surprise now, would it?"

My whole class went "Oooo!"

I thought the man would explode. You could practically see the steam shooting out his ears. He pulled a ruler out of his back pocket, and all my eighth graders leaned forward, assuming we were getting ready to rumble.

I would not be intimidated. "Are you planning on hitting me with that thing?"

"No, no, no, no," he said. "I'm not going to strike you, but I am going to ask you to put a foot up here on the top of your desk."

"May I ask why?"

"I discovered footprints on the lab tables, and I'm about to measure your shoe."

I glanced toward the girl in the orange jumpsuit and she said, "No way! He needs a warrant for that!"

I said to Mr. Barnes, "I have it on sound legal advice that you need a warrant for that."

He shoved the ruler back into his hip pocket as he barked, "I think you know more about this, but you're not willing to say."

I replied, "I can neither deny nor confirm that statement."

He spun around on his heel and walked out just as the bell rang. The hall flooded with kids. I jumped into the stream, hiding myself from Mr. Barnes and using students as a human shield. I made my way through the crowd and down the hall to the science lab. I told Debbie everything that had happened and she said, "Oh, you got him to write something? That's great! But we can do better. Go down to the gym and get Brian."

I went to the gym, pulled a kid out of PE, and brought him back to the science lab. Brian was a little guy. He hadn't hit his growth spurt anywhere but in his mouth. He talked all the time. I remember getting so frustrated with him one day and yelling, "Brian, when you die, we're going to have to dig you up and kill your tongue!"

Debbie said to Brian, "I'm all the time fussing at you for climbing on the furniture. Now's your chance. Climb up here and help us pull down all this mess."

Brian jumped up on the tables and started tearing down the streamers of toilet paper. While we were cleaning up, Debbie let it slip that it was Hood who had done it. This was a stroke of genius, because big-mouth Brian immediately blabbed the secret to everybody, and by lunchtime Hood was the hero of the eighth grade. I stood in the hallway during the change of classes and watched kids congratulating him with high fives and slaps on the back. Later that afternoon, Debbie brought the celebration to a happy end by wrapping Hood's chair with toilet paper before he came into science class. He took one look at his seat and started to grin. Everyone had a good laugh.

At the end of the day, after I had spent another ninety minutes tutoring Hood and his mom had taken him home, I heard a familiar low growl at my classroom door. Mr. Barnes said, "Would you please come here?"

"Yes, sir."

He was rocking back and forth on his heels with his hands behind his back. He began a new interrogation. "Toilet paper, huh?"

"Yes, sir."

"That's taxpayer money, you know?"

"Yes, sir, I know."

"You got him to write an essay?"

"Yes, I did."

He stopped rocking and eyed me up and down for just a second. Then he reached out to shake my hand. But he reached out left-handed. I know it seems like I'm making this up, but it's the honest-to-goodness truth. Mr. Barnes always extended his left hand for a handshake because, just like Hood, he was born with four stubs and a thumb on his right hand.

He gripped extra hard and held on long enough to say, "You did a really good thing for that boy." Then he released my hand to reassume the stance of a pit bull as he said, "Next time, just do it in somebody else's building."

ATTENDING CHURCH

THE BOSS OF THIS CHURCH

Since it was the Bicentennial of the United States, my mother had dressed the entire family appropriately. I was wearing white alligator shoes, blue pants, and a bright red jacket. My bright white shirt was buttoned up to my Adam's apple and accessorized with a clip-on red, white, and blue bowtie large enough to frame my entire face. I looked like a four-foot Lawrence Welk. My sister, Joy, was wearing a bright red dress with white anklet socks and navy-blue patent leather Mary Janes. My mom had on a very conservative navy-blue dress with a bright red scarf. My dad was also dressed conservatively in a navy suit, but he was sporting an American flag necktie at least six inches wide and tied with a knot the size of a volleyball. Before we got into the car, my mother checked her hair, then made sure Dad had a handkerchief in his pocket and that my sister and I both had a quarter to put in the offering basket because we were on our way to church.

But this wasn't just any regular Sunday church service. On this particular 1976 Sunday, my dad was candidating at Putney Bible Baptist Church in Harlan, Kentucky. He had been invited to preach a model sermon and stay afterward for a business meeting in which the membership would decide whether to issue an official call to become their new pastor. As my mom put my sister and me into the back seat of the car, she reminded us to be on our best behavior because we were attending a worship service, it was our patriotic duty, and Daddy really needed this job!

Upon our arrival we were given a tour of the building, which didn't take more than ten minutes since it was a small country church, nothing fancy. Very soon, it was time for the service to begin. My mom sat on the aisle, third row, right side. My mom always sat on the aisle, third row, right side; I always sat next to her; Joy sat next to me; and finally, Joy's little boy, Tom Junior, sat next to her.

My little sister was only three years old, but she was already a mother. By the time she was ten years old, Joy had over a hundred children in her baby doll collection. Even though he wasn't the most talented, Tom Junior was her favorite. He didn't talk like Chatty Cathy, he didn't go pee-pee like Baby Alive, he didn't grow hair like the red-headed Crissy doll. In fact, he was smooth-headed and his hair was painted on. Tom Junior's only distinctive feature was that he had no fingers on his left hand, just a big hole where the plastic molded fingers were supposed to be. Joy had accidentally closed the car door on has hand and chopped them off. She would put band-aids over the hole and say, "Don't make fun of Tom Junior. He's handicapped." She doted on that doll like the perfect little mommy.

A family friend, who worked as an obstetrics nurse, had given my sister a diaper bag for Tom Junior filled with hospital samples: bottles, preemie diapers, baby lotion, everything a mother might need. We had another friend who was a Bible salesman. He had given my dad a sample New Testament. When he offered to have the little blue book personalized, Dad had Tom Junior's name embossed in gold on the bottom corner of the front cover. Joy always made sure Tom Junior's Bible was tucked into his diaper bag when she took him to church. When my dad began the sermon, she would take out the little New Testament and turn a few pages, pretending to locate the text for her child. Then she would lay it in Tom Junior's lap so he could follow along. About halfway through my dad's thirty-minute sermon, she would pretend Tom Junior was being disruptive as she reached over to jab him with a finger and hiss in a church whisper, "Be quiet!" Joy and Tom Junior were quite the show. Looking back on that time, I dare say some people came to church to hear my dad preach and other people came just to watch Joy discipline Tom Junior.

On this special Sunday, my dad was working hard to make a good impression. Making sure he said everything that needed to be said, his sermon was running long. This was not a particular problem for Tom Junior. He was sitting very still. But when I glanced over at his mommy, she was wiggling in the church pew. The longer my dad preached, the more Joy wiggled.

Finally, I leaned over and whispered, "The bathroom is downstairs."

I remembered the location from our brief tour of the church building. To get to the toilet from where we were seated, you had to walk to the back of the church where fourteen stairs descended into the basement. After going down the steep steps and finding yourself beneath the church sanctuary, you had to cross the entire concrete floor to find a little one-holer tucked away in the far corner. By the time you locked yourself into that tiny bathroom, you were situated directly below the pulpit upstairs. Because the plumbing was so loud, someone had hung a little sign above the commode that read, "Do not flush during sermon." I suppose this was a polite way of reminding folks that any loud sound from the bathroom would be heard by the entire congregation when there was only the preacher's voice to cover any noise. If making a noise was unavoidable, it was best to wait until the organ was playing an anthem. (I never really thought about it, but the old hymn "The Trumpet Shall Sound" suddenly comes to mind.)

My sister took Tom Junior by the hand and slipped out the far end of the pew. I knew she was on her way to the bathroom when I heard Tom Junior's head clonking on every step as she made her way down the stairs, but nobody else seemed to notice. A few minutes later, my mother turned her attention away from my dad's sermon long enough to check on us kids and realized Joy and Tom Junior were gone. She raised an eyebrow at me, her silent way of asking, "Where is your sister?"

I never got the chance to respond, because Joy answered for herself. My sister was, for the most part, very independent. She managed to find the bathroom all by herself, but being only three years old she needed some assistance with "the paperwork." My dad's sermon was interrupted by a little voice calling out from the basement, "Mommy! Come wipe my tail!" Instantly, my mother's face turned redder than the scarf tied around her neck. She stood and turned to exit the sanctuary. She was facing pretty much the entire congregation when Joy added, "I already wiped Tom Junior! He's fine!"

My mother walked out of the sanctuary, down the stairs, into the basement, and locked herself in the bathroom with Joy and Tom Junior while my dad valiantly continued preaching as if nothing had happened. When the service ended, he and I joined the rest of the family in the basement to wait while the congregation conducted their business meeting upstairs. We sat very still and quiet. Even though the meeting was supposed to be private, we heard every word. There was some discussion about the sermon and a little back and forth, which made it hard to tell how the majority of the congregation felt.

Then we heard a female voice say, "Well, I thought the sermon was excellent. Plus, he managed to preach through distractions and simultaneously proved his children are normal. As our former pastor has retired, I move we issue a call for Reverend Lowry to be the next full-time minister of Putney Bible Baptist Church." Apparently, whoever this woman was, her opinion carried a lot of weight because the vote was immediate and unanimous.

Our whole family was asked to come back upstairs so the church could greet us properly. We learned the lady who had spoken on my sister's behalf was named Helen Gemberling, but all the Sunday school kids called her Miss Gem for short. Miss Gem had taught Sunday school at Putney Bible Baptist Church for more than thirty-seven years. Everyone knew and respected her, and it didn't take me long to figure out why. I got a clue when one of the Sunday school kids told me, "If Miss Gem catches you chewing gum, not only will you never chew gum in church again, you probably won't chew gum anymore, anywhere, for the rest of your life!"

On that first Sunday at our new church, when Miss Gem extended the right hand of fellowship to my father, she leaned in as they shook hands and said, "Pastor, a word."

"Yes, Miss Gem, what's on your mind?"

"Now that we have a full-time leader for our congregation, I wonder if the first order of business shouldn't be for you to organize a group of ladies to serve as nursery volunteers and care for the babies during your preaching. I was particularly thinking of little ones like, um, Tom Junior."

My dad smiled as he agreed. "Oh certainly, Miss Gem, I think we can do that."

By the next Sunday, my dad had recruited a couple ladies to take the babies to the church basement during the sermon. My sister sent Tom Junior with one of the volunteers and told her if he started fussing, to just let him cry it out.

A few weeks later I got to know Miss Gem better when my dad conducted his first communion service. As a little kid, I didn't really understand what a communion service meant, but the words my dad spoke were very familiar to me. When he served the bread, which was actually saltine crackers, he would quote the words of Jesus saying, "This is my body, which is broken for you." Then before the ushers distributed the little glasses of grape juice he would say, "This is my blood, which is poured out for you." To be completely honest, I might have understood it a little better if I had paused to give it more thought, but I was always anxiously waiting for the communion service to be over because I wanted to get my hands on the little glasses of grape juice that were left over. I liked to shoot them back like the cowboys with their whiskey shots from *Gunsmoke.*

After the service had ended and the congregation was dismissed, I had just bellied up to the communion table to gulp my first mouthful of juice when I heard an authoritative voice behind me say, "Young man, put that down!"

I turned around to see Miss Gem staring down at me like US Marshal Matt Dillon eyeballing a bad guy. I very slowly lowered my shot glass and stepped away from the communion table. Instead of drawing a firearm, Miss Gem reached into the sleeve of her sweater to extract a fancy handkerchief to spread out like a little tablecloth on the communion table. Then she picked up the silver tray of saltine crackers and dumped them onto the handkerchief. After folding the cloth into a little bag, she lifted her ample elbow and came down on the handkerchief like a man getting ready to arm wrestle, crushing the crackers into little bits. With one hand she picked up the bag of crumbs and with the other the tray filled with communion shot glasses.

"Follow me."

My sister had also been watching. She grabbed Tom Junior and the three of us followed our new Sunday school teacher out the back door and into the graveyard. Miss Gem turned toward us and explained, "These elements have been set aside for a sacred purpose and we do not play with them. I will pour the extra grape juice onto the flowers for a little added moisture. You may sprinkle these crumbs onto the graves." When my sister asked why, Miss Gem continued. "The birds will come to peck at the crumbs. When they fly heavenward, we are reminded that our loved ones buried here will be resurrected on the last day when the trumpet sounds. Then we that remain shall be caught up together to meet them in the clouds. And so shall we ever be with the Lord."

My sister looked at me and said, "Dang! Our daddy is the new preacher, but she's the boss of this church!"

And over the years of growing up at Putney Bible Baptist Church, we came to realize just how accurate my sister's statement had been. Miss Gem built Putney Bible

Baptist Church, literally, with her bare hands. As a young woman attending Bible college in Pennsylvania, she had dedicated her life to missionary work, assuming that after graduating with a seminary degree she would serve on foreign shores. But in those days, a mission board wouldn't send a single woman to the wilds of Borneo, so she came to the mountains of Kentucky instead. In many respects, it was pretty much the same thing. A great deal of strength and determination was required.

Miss Gem began her work by starting a Sunday school for children, hosting classes in her own home. When enough adults showed interest, a committee secured a plot of land on which to build a proper church. Miss Gem helped with the physical construction. Local folks told the story of the day when she arrived at the construction site with a large basket full of sandwiches for the volunteer workers. The men were constructing a high cinderblock wall, and a burly mountain man named Hagar Johnson was struggling to lift a fifty-pound sack of mortar mix. Miss Gem stepped over to him and said, "Oh, my dear young man, may I be of assistance?" She handed him the basket full of sandwiches, hefted the sack onto her shoulder, ran it up the ladder, and plopped it down atop the wall. Hagar Johnson was so ashamed a missionary woman from Pennsylvania could out-lift him he never came to church again.

Not only was Miss Gem stronger than many men, but she could wield a gun better than most. Folks told another story about a hot, summer evening when a couple whip-poorwills were making a racket and keeping Miss Gem from sleeping. She got up, threw a single shell into her shotgun, stepped out onto the porch, and dispatched both birds with a single shot. And lest you think it was cruel of her to shoot those birds, you should know it was rumored that some moonshiners happened to be cutting across the far end of her yard at the edge of the woods. When they saw firsthand how the missionary lady was a crack shot, they stayed well away from her property. The whippoorwills were a blessing in disguise.

After Miss Gem took us to the graveyard to properly dispose of the communion elements, she found my dad and said, "Pastor, a word."

"Yes, Miss Gem, what can I do for you?"

"I wonder if we couldn't start a junior church service so children could be taught about various traditions—baptism, communion, those types of things. Perhaps you could find some volunteers willing to instruct the children?"

Miss Gem had asked it like a question, but my dad knew it was really more of a command. However, it wasn't a bad idea. He and some of the men built a partition in the church basement, so one side could be used as a nursery and the other could host a junior church service while the adults worshipped in the sanctuary upstairs.

Though she could be rather stern, Miss Gem was also very generous. If you did her a favor or helped her with chores at her home, she didn't just thank you with a pat on the back or a "God bless you." She did those things, but also gave you a great, big, full-size Hershey bar. Consequently, we Sunday school kids were always looking for an excuse to help Miss Gem around her house, which was just across the road and up a steep hill from the church.

One snowy day, when I was about ten, school was canceled due to the bad weather. My sister and I had gone with my dad to the church to play in the sanctuary while he wrote sermons at his desk in a little side room. Playing church was fun for a little while, but I soon got bored. Joy had her baby dolls to keep her busy, but I was looking for something to do when the mailman stopped by on his rounds. He mentioned to my dad that his vehicle couldn't make it up Miss Gem's icy driveway to deliver her mail. I immediately volunteered to take her mail up the hill, anticipating the customary Hershey bar. My dad said that would be fine, and the mailman handed me a stack of envelopes, a newspaper, and a *National Geographic* magazine, all bound together with a thick rubber band.

I put on my coat, gloves, and hat and started out. Walking across the road from the church was easy, but Miss Gem's icy driveway was like trying to climb Mount Everest. I was wearing slick-bottomed cowboy boots, and every time I struggled about ten feet up the hill I began to slide back down. Finally, I resorted to crawling up her steep driveway, which took the better part of an hour, but I was determined to get myself a Hershey bar. When I knocked on Miss Gem's door, she opened it to find me shivering like a cold dog in a wet sack, her mail a complete mess.

"Oh, dear me! It's a wonder if you haven't suffered frostbite." She took the soggy mail from my hand and ushered me through the door into her living room. After pulling off my soggy gloves, hat, and coat, she plopped me into a chair and got down onto her knees to pull off my cowboy boots and my soaking wet socks. My feet were red and raw, and for some reason I was embarrassed she was rubbing my bare feet. Miss Gem could see I was uncomfortable. She stood up and walked into the kitchen. A few minutes later she came back with a pan of warm water, set it on the floor in front of me and said, "Here, put your feet in this warm water and I won't be able to see them." Well, it was the most ridiculous thing to say, because the water was clear, but when I put my feet into the pan it felt so good I forgot to be self-conscious. Then she said, "Now, you're going to want something to do," as she handed me a pair of binoculars that had been sitting on a little table next to my chair. "Here, take these and watch the birds."

Mounted on a pole outside her picture window was a large bird feeder next to a dark hemlock tree. I believe every native bird from the Kentucky mountains was either on that feeder or perched in the branches of that great evergreen. Through the binoculars I studied cardinals, finches, juncos, chickadees, and the occasional bluejay. However, I didn't mention the bluejays to Miss Gem because she hated them. She didn't appreciate the way they aggressively chased all the other birds away from the feeder, picking and pecking at their rivals. Referencing the story of Adam and Eve's original sin, she said bluejays were a result of the Fall, nothing more than glorified crows, and she would not tolerate them. In fact, when I was a little older, I learned bigger boys earned their spending money for Bible camp with their BB guns. Miss Gem would give them a dollar for every dead bluejay they brought to her door. However, she didn't give me money for delivering her mail, just the expected Hershey bar. She also let me look at the *National Geographic* magazine. It was all about the animal research scientist Jane Goodall and her work with chimpanzees and the great apes. I suppose Miss Gem telephoned my dad at the church, because after a while he came to get me in a borrowed four-wheel-drive Jeep that could easily make it up her driveway.

I had enjoyed a delightful afternoon with Miss Gem. I was so taken with her binoculars and bird feeder my dad suggested we put up one of our own to observe the birds' feeding habits as a science project for school. I kept a notebook by our living room window and wrote down what time of day different birds came to the feeder. There were multiples of each species, and I needed some way to differentiate between the first cardinal, and the second cardinal, and so on. Remembering how Jane Goodall named the apes she studied, I did the same thing, but there were so many birds, I quickly ran out of names.

My dad, being a preacher, flopped open the family Bible that always lay on our coffee table and said, "Let me introduce you to the genealogies."

After that I would copy names out of the Bible. There was a pair of cardinals named Abraham and Sarah, and a second pair named Isaac and Rebekah. Cardinals were easy to name, because they always came in pairs, but there were way too many chickadees flocking around the feeder to give each bird an individual name so I would just note in my journal "Children of Israel feeding at 4:00 pm." I was very proud of my work, and I took my journal to Sunday school to show it to Miss Gem.

She took time to study the pages and brag on my note-taking, then she said to my dad, "Pastor, a word."

By this time, my dad had learned this always meant more work for him, but he patiently said, "Yes, Miss Gem, what are you thinking?"

"I wonder if the church couldn't host a junior boys and girls club. Kind of like the scouts, but with more of a spiritual emphasis, so our young people could learn about God's wonderful creation."

By spring, we had kids signed up for club meetings, and Miss Gem even taught a riflery class.

Delivering Miss Gem's mail turned out to be the beginning of my lifelong love for nature—birdwatching in particular—but it wasn't the only memorable visit to her home. My sister and I loved going there, and most of our memories have to do with snow or Christmas.

When we were still little kids, Miss Gem came to us one Sunday in December before the evening prayer service and said, "I want to invite you to my house after church to watch the Christmas specials on my color television."

Wow! What a treat! Not only did we get to see *Rudolph the Red-Nosed Reindeer* and *Frosty the Snowman* in living color, but Miss Gem's television had a remote control! I suppose other people had a store-bought remote control, but Miss Gem had made her own by removing the back cover of her set to access the circuitry. She ran a long cable from the television speaker across the floor to a light switch on the little table by her chair. She couldn't use her switch to change the channels, but she could turn the sound off during the commercials, preferring the silence to what she called "worldly trash."

However, when the Christmas specials aired, all the commercials were for toys, and we wanted to hear them. She made a game of it by turning off the sound and asking us to sing the jingles. I remember singing, "Lite Brite! Lite Brite! Turn on the magic of colored light. Lite Brite! Lite Brite! Make a picture to glow at night. Lite Brite by Milton Bradley!" The very next Sunday when we went to our car in the church parking lot, we opened the door to find a brand-new Lite Brite anonymously placed in the backseat.

My sister said, "Oh look! Santa Claus came to church!" But my daddy said, "I think Santa Claus looks a lot like a certain Sunday School teacher we know."

The Lite Brite was very special, but it was not the most memorable gift Miss Gem ever bestowed upon an unsuspecting family. Not by a long shot! It might have been that same year, I was certainly very young, when we were visiting Miss Gem and my dad asked to use her bathroom. After just a minute or so, he opened the bathroom door and called to me, "Timmy, come here." I went to him, and he said, "Come into the bathroom."

"I don't have to go."

He repeated his directive. "Come into the bathroom."

"I don't even have to try."

"I don't want you to try, there's something I need to show you."

I stepped into the bathroom and my dad raised the toilet seat to reveal a zigzagging line running all the way around the underside of the ring. I had no idea what I was looking at until my dad explained. "Miss Gem enjoys a heated toilet seat. She has wired a heating coil to the underside of her toilet seat and she plugs it into the wall." Then my dad said in a very serious tone, "Never get this wet, because if you do you will light up like a Christmas tree." After that, while my sister and I were watching television, I heard him mention this unique invention to Miss Gem.

Just a few days later at the Christmas Eve service, Miss Gem said to my dad, "Pastor, a word." He was afraid to answer, so she continued. "I know we usually give each person a sack of candy with an orange and an apple after the Christmas Eve service, but this year I have something special."

Miss Gem had gone to the hardware store, purchased seventeen toilet seats, wired them with heating coils, and proudly presented one to each family after we finished singing "Silent Night."

During another Christmas season we went to visit Miss Gem and discovered that instead of decorating with traditional ornaments, she had placed lava lamps on every flat surface in her living room. With all those globes bubbling orange, blue, green, and purple blobs, we were a bit surprised to hear traditional Christmas carols playing on her radio; sitar music seemed more in keeping with the atmosphere. She proudly informed us she had bought them for "next to nothing" in the local thrift store. My dad didn't have the heart to tell her the police had given all those lava lamps to the store after a drug bust at a local opium den. After she read about the crime in the newspaper and put two and two together, she picked up the telephone and called my dad.

"Pastor, a word. I wonder if we couldn't start a youth group for the teenagers of our community, so they'd have something more constructive to do with their time."

Miss Gem spoke and it was so. The teens in our church had all known Miss Gem as their Sunday School teacher from their earliest childhood days, so seeing something new come into being merely because she mentioned it seemed only natural. They knew she wasn't divine but assumed she was pretty darn close.

However, I knew Miss Gem wasn't perfect. She had a secret passion: Monday Night Football. She loved the sport, and she more than loved the players. Particularly the Pittsburg Steelers. I never was a football fan, but occasionally I would sit down and watch a game with Miss Gem. If you were listening closely, you could hear her whisper under her breath when one of her favorite players took the field, "Look at that fine specimen of a man." If her version of "fantasy football" was as close as Miss Gem ever got to one of the seven deadly sins, I was willing to give her some grace.

When I was a teenager and part of the youth group started at Miss Gem's suggestion, the phone rang one snowy day. It was Miss Gem asking for my dad's help. He assumed her driveway was icy and she needed someone to bring up the mail, but she informed him that a neighbor had shoveled her drive earlier that morning. The issue was the pilot light had gone out on her furnace, and she couldn't get it relit. I volunteered to go with my dad, grabbing my coat, hat, and gloves without even thinking about the Hershey bar that was sure to be mine. By this time, I had learned the rewards of visiting Miss Gem were always more interesting and sweeter than any chocolate bar.

As our car came to the top of her hill, we were surprised to see Miss Gem standing outside, holding onto a porch post with blood all around her on the snow. It wasn't very much blood, but when you see even just a little bit of red on bright white snow, it's quite shocking.

I jumped out of the car saying, "Miss Gem, you're hurt."

She quickly assured me. "Oh, don't worry about the blood, dear young man. It's merely a flesh wound. My driveway, as you know, is clear, but I came out to pour some salt on the steps. I seem to remember a boy who once had quite a time with his slippery cowboy boots. As these things happen, I was the one who slipped. I tried to catch myself by grabbing hold of the railing and I cut my hand a little bit. However, my leg simply doesn't belong to me."

I realized one of her legs was visibly shorter than the other. She was holding onto the porch post to keep from putting weight on it. An x-ray would eventually confirm the suspicion that she had broken her hip.

My dad asked, "Miss Gem, how can we help you?"

Even though she must have been in a great deal of pain, she still took full charge of the situation. "Go into the house and get a straight-back chair from the kitchen."

We were loath to do it, but she insisted on sitting down on her broken hip so we could carry her into the house. I'm telling you, no Pittsburgh Steeler was ever that tough. By the time we got her inside she was very pale. Her lips were blue and trembling. She grabbed my dad by the arm and said, "Call the Holbrook Home for Funerals."

"Miss Gem, I'm a little concerned about you going into shock, but I don't think you are going to die."

"I don't think I'm going to die either, but the owner, Mr. Holbrook, attended my Sunday school when he was a boy. They run an excellent ambulance service. Call the funeral home and they will take me to the hospital."

Once again, my dad followed her very clear orders.

After the EMS workers had her on a gurney and were about to lift her into the back of the ambulance, Miss Gem raised a hand and said, "Pastor, a word." My dad leaned forward to hear one final instruction. "No need to come to the hospital. I'm fine. But after you have relit my pilot light, do feed the birds."

After the ambulance pulled away, I looked at my dad and said, "You messed up."

He was incredulous. "How did I mess up? I did everything she told me to do."

"That's exactly my point. If you hadn't leaned in to hear that final order, they would've put her into the ambulance and driven off to the hospital, and you would've finally been the boss of our church."

My dad raised his eyes toward the sky. "You and I both know I actually answer to another Boss, but don't tell Miss Gem that."

Miss Gem recovered well and came right back home to pick up where she had left off. After I graduated from high school, my family moved to South Carolina, but my dad didn't worry about Putney Bible Baptist Church. He left the congregation in more-than-capable hands. A few years later, when the call came letting us know Miss Gem had died, my dad was informed she had wanted him to officiate at her burial. When we arrived at Holbrook's Home for Funerals to go over the arrangements, Mr. Holbrook himself handed Dad an envelope containing her written instructions. With my hand to heaven, I half expected her last request to begin "Pastor, a word ..."

The funeral home chapel was overflowing. Every person attending could tell a story, several stories, about the missionary lady from Pennsylvania who built Putney Bible Baptist Church. And we will continue telling stories about her until the last day when the trumpet shall sound, then we who remain shall be caught up together to meet Miss Gem in the clouds. I am completely confident of that fact every time I hear the pastor quote THE Boss of THE Church during a communion service and remember her standing there in the snow.

"This is my body which is broken for you. This is my blood which is poured out for you." Because of those words, I can confidently tell my own children, just as Miss Gem told me, "And so shall we ever be with the Lord."

NOT IN THE BIBLE, BUT IT SHOULD BE

I'm an Anglican now, but I was raised a Baptist. I switched over for fear of deep water. My daddy is a Baptist preacher. Consequently, I went to church all the time. Never missed a service. As a child, I remember laying on the couch with a fever of 102, with the television remote control in my hand, suffering a moral dilemma. I was too sick to go to Sunday evening service, so would it be a sin to watch *The Wonderful World of Disney*? I never got to see that program because we were always at church. Beginning with Sunday school at ten, Sundays were filled with church activities until seven or eight at night.

Sunday School was not the most exciting thing I had ever experienced. It was certainly no *Wonderful World of Disney*. Probably because it was so overly familiar. There was the toddler class, the beginner class, the junior class, the middle school class, and finally the high school class. After you completed all of those you were recruited to teach the children coming up behind you.

It was always the same thing, year after year. The first Sunday after Labor Day we began with Adam and Eve. By Christmas, Jesus had been born. By May we were studying the end of the world in the Book of Revelation. Same thing over and over. No surprises. Like that old Sunday School joke where the teacher says, "Boys and girls, this Sunday I have a wonderful story for you. It's about a little fuzzy animal with a long, fluffy tail that lives in a tree and eats nuts. What do you think it is?" A little boy raises his hand and says, "Sounds like a squirrel to me, but I know the answer has got to be Jesus." That's what it was like in my Sunday School.

When I was a kid there was a country music singer named Ray Stevens. He wrote a song called "The Mississippi Squirrel Revival" about these ornery boys that took a squirrel to church in a shoe box. It got loose and went running up people's pant legs. The service was interrupted by folks jumping up and shouting. Everybody thought it was the Holy Spirit, but actually it was just a crazy squirrel. We Sunday School kids loved that song. We prayed for a squirrel, a bobcat, a Tasmanian devil, anything that would liven up those Sunday mornings.

God is very gracious, and the scripture says he does not give in a chintzy fashion. No, no, the scripture says he gives pressed down, shaken together, and running over. We didn't get a bobcat or a squirrel or a Tasmanian devil. We got a three-headed monster named Todd, Spencer, and Jerry.

The whole thing started with the star chart. Baptists count everything. And when you're in Sunday School, the count is kept on the star chart. Displayed on the wall of every Sunday School room was a big poster with a column of children's names down the left side. There were rows of little squares out from everybody's name where the teacher marked each item with a gold star: Bibles brought, lessons completed, verses memorized, visitors attending, and offering money collected. All the Sunday School teachers kept careful records. When you went into the worship service there was a board above the piano on the left side and a board above the organ on the right side. They had little slide-in letters and numbers like a theater marquee. It was here that all the weekly statistics from every Sunday School class were compiled and posted for the entire congregation to review. The total offering money collected was most prominent, with a column for offering collected today and a column for offering collected one year ago. The congregation wanted to see an increase year over year when it came to the amount collected. I kept a sharp eye on that particular tabulation because my daddy was the preacher, and unless there was an increase, we were not going on a family vacation. So that was a constant matter of prayer.

I always had a perfect constellation of gold stars next to my name on the Sunday School class chart. I was the preacher's kid—I never missed anything. I used to sit in the worship service and listen to the adults sing that old gospel song about soul winning. "Will there be any stars, any stars in your crown? Any stars when the sun goeth down?" I used to think, *I don't know about my crown, but I got more points on my star chart than Jeane Dixon!*

But my Sunday School teacher noticed a row that was conspicuously empty—visitors attending. And of course, the row next to it—souls saved. She figured there was a correlation. It was her theory that if we could get more children to visit Sunday School, their souls would be saved, and we could give them a gold star and count them among the righteous. So she went to my daddy, with the idea of a visitor drive, sort of a contest. There would be prizes and incentives if you brought a friend to Sunday School.

My dad was all for it and he asked me if I knew any kids who might be interested. As it happened, I attended elementary school with three brothers named Todd, Spencer, and Jerry. Actually, by birth order, they were Spencer, Todd, and Jerry. But Todd was the most gregarious. I suppose he was the most assertive because he was the middle child. You know how it is. The oldest demands attention, the baby is spoiled rotten, but the one in the middle is all on his own.

Todd served as sort of the spokesman for the trio and he was my classmate in school. Spencer was a grade ahead and Jerry was a grade behind. These boys were famous at my school the way gangsters are famous, or perhaps the way a particularly destructive hurricane is remembered in the annals of history. But I didn't mention that to my dad, I just told him the school bus picked them up from the trailer park about halfway between our church and the elementary school. My dad immediately made a plan to go visit the family and invite them to church.

We got to those boys just in the nick of time. The week we decided to visit their home, each boy had done something at school that made it plain a moral influence was much needed. Monday, Spencer got his mouth washed out with soap for saying "sex" to a kindergartner. On Tuesday, Todd got a paddling because he bounced a seesaw on a little boy's head and made him bleed. On Wednesday, Jerry was sent home early because he brought an inappropriate magazine to Show and Tell. Thursday there was an altercation on the playground, but when the principal realized they were just fighting amongst themselves, he didn't do anything about it because he was hoping the three brothers would kill each other and he'd be rid of the whole mess.

When my daddy mentioned to the principal that we were going to invite the brothers to Sunday School, he gave my dad a look and said, "I'm a Methodist, but we'll pray for all of you good folks at the Baptist church."

We were going to call Thursday evening because that's when Baptists do visitation. Baptists call on Thursdays, usually after the six o'clock news, but before something nasty starts showing on HBO. If you're watching the second puzzle on *Wheel of Fortune* and there's a knock at your door, it's a Baptist. In the middle of the day, that's when the Jehovah's Witnesses call. They are prone to interrupt a housewife's soap opera viewing schedule, but the Baptists call in the evening. We always made official visits in the church bus, which was actually a fifteen-passenger van. Your church might have one of these. The church's name and logo was painted on the side, and a volunteer would drive around picking up folks who didn't have a ride to church or bringing kids from the trailer park to the Sunday School. This transportation service was commonly called the "Church Bus Ministry," which is taken from the biblical Greek for "hell on wheels."

As we turned off the main road into the trailer park we realized we didn't know which trailer belonged to Todd, Spencer, and Jerry's family, but we soon spotted them. The three boys were huddled around the front steps of the little porch attached to their trailer. My dad parked the van. He climbed out one side and I hopped out the other. As soon as they saw us, they all stood up and spoke.

Todd said, "Hey, Preacher!"

Then Spencer echoed, "Look! It's the preacher!"

Jerry, the littlest one, held up his Polaroid camera. I don't know where he got it or why he carried it, but he always had that thing hanging by a strap around his neck. It was like a plastic security blanket; he was never without it. Aiming the camera, Jerry said, "Hey, Preacher! You want me to take your picture?"

My daddy said, "No, no, Jerry, you know me. You see me all the time. Don't take a picture of me. I don't want you to waste your film."

Jerry put the camera back down. Then they sort of parted like the Red Sea to show us what they had been huddled over. Laying on the porch step before us was a dead squirrel tacked with four nails, all splayed out like a taxidermy specimen.

Spencer brandished a pocketknife. "We're going to play surgery!"

Jerry added, "I'm going to take a picture of it."

I thought to myself, *That's why we never had a Mississippi squirrel in my Sunday School—Todd, Spencer, and Jerry killed it!*

My dad stepped over the carcass and asked, "Boys, is your mother home?"

"Yeah, she's in there," they chimed together. And as we walked up on the porch they yelled, "Mom! The preacher's here!"

They left the squirrel and followed us up the steps. Dad knocked on the door of the trailer and we were greeted by a cacophony of Chihuahua barks. Then we heard a female voice holler, "Come in, come on in! Door's open!"

My dad opened the door and a big blue cloud of cigarette smoke wafted out onto the porch as we stepped into a dimly lit living room with Todd, Spencer, and Jerry trailing behind. There must have been at least eight little dogs jumping on the couch. Now my daddy was prepared for the Chihuahuas. He was wearing his cowboy boots. He always wore cowboy boots on Thursday night visitation. Once I asked him about that and he said, "When those nasty little suckers come running out from under the furniture and try to bite you on the ankles, with one swift kick you can send them straight on to Glory."

When Todd, Spencer, and Jerry's momma stood up to greet my dad, a whole lap blanket of canine slid off her knees and ran under the dust ruffle of the couch. Once the dogs were hidden away she said, "Hey, Preacher, I know you. My boys go to school with your boy. Here, let me get you a seat." She started moving newspapers and magazines off the couch. There was a half-eaten peanut butter and jelly sandwich laying on a chair. She shoved it toward my father and said, "Would you like a snack?" When my dad declined, she stuffed it under the couch where the Chihuahuas started scrapping over the treat. She sat back down, leaned forward and hollered under the couch to the dogs. "Settle down! And when you get done with that sandwich, I want you to get back to business."

She sat back up and noticed a questioning look on my daddy's face. "Oh, you wonder what I'm talking about? Not all these dogs is mine. I got a real purty female and my neighbor's got a real purty male. We got a business transaction going on underneath the couch. We're going to split the proceeds from selling my dog's puppies." Then she raised the dust ruffle and shouted, "How's it going under there?" My dad looked horrified when she took a drag on her cigarette and said to the dogs with a chuckle, "When y'all get her done, I'll let you have a smoke."

My dad looked at me. "Why don't you go play with Todd, Spencer, and Jerry?"

I knew my cue. When your daddy is the Baptist preacher and he says "Go play with your friends," that's code for "Keep these kids busy while I try to convert their heathen mother." So I said, "Do y'all have a game we could play?"

They shouted, "Oh yeah, we have a game. Come on, come on, we'll play our game." The boys ran down the little narrow hallway to the back end of the trailer and I followed.

Now I was a little innocent Baptist kid, about second grade at the time, and I was thinking they probably had Monopoly, Clue, a board game of one type or another. Oh, no, no, no, nothing like that. We went into the master bedroom of the trailer and were immediately confronted with a big, long dresser just inside the door. There was a mirror up one side, and the top of that dresser was littered with cans of Aqua Net hairspray, bottles of Rose Milk hand lotion, a family size bag of M&M's candy, and a styrofoam head with a big blonde bouffant wig jammed on it. There was a smoking curling iron somebody had forgotten to unplug. In the middle of all that sat a big Hi-Fi stereo.

One of the boys said, "This is our new game we made up!" Jerry lifted the lid of the stereo and flipped on the turntable to forty-five speed so that it was spinning around really fast. Todd and Spencer pulled off their shoes and jumped up onto the bed, which pretty much filled the rest of the room and was covered in slick red satin sheets. They started bouncing up and down like clowns on a trampoline. "This is our game. Watch, watch!"

Jerry, the one with the Polaroid camera, grabbed the bag of M&Ms, stuck his hand down in it, came up with a fistful of candies, and hurled them onto the spinning record player. The candies shot across the room in every direction.

Todd, still bouncing on the bed, said, "If you get hit, you're out!"

I looked across the bed and saw chocolate pockmarks all over the wall. It looked like somebody had shot a candy machine gun across the room! Jerry tossed a few more candies onto the turntable and one hit Spencer right in the face. He used the back of his hand to wipe off the M&M stuck to his forehead. "It's a green one. I'll take the wig."

They looked at me. Obviously I didn't know the rules of the game. Spencer stopped jumping long enough to explain. "If you get hit with a green one, you're a girl. If you get hit with a red one, you're dead and there ain't nothing you can do about it."

He licked the chocolate off his hand. Jerry threw him the wig and he jammed it on his head. They went back to bouncing up and down on the bed. Suddenly, one of them slipped on the red satin sheets and banged against the wall, knocking the black velvet portrait of Elvis hanging over the bed down to the floor. *Bam!* All three boys froze like statues.

We heard their mama yell, "You better not mess up that picture of my boyfriend!"

They looked at me and whispered, "We gotta go!" Grabbing their shoes they slipped out the back door.

I was following them when I heard my daddy yell, "Don't go too far!"

Oh, it was too late. I had already gone way too far. My world was sane, ordered, and biblical. Theirs was crazy, chaotic, and fraught with physical danger!

Outside we heard a train blowing its horn. Todd, Spencer, and Jerry took off running across a field adjacent to the trailer park shouting, "Come on, come on!"

The train track ran right through the middle of the county where I grew up. Everybody lived on one side or the other. All us kids would run to the edge of our yards and wave to the train. Sometimes the engineers would wave back and give an extra blast on the horn. I thought that's what we were going to do. But when we reached the top of a bank overlooking the railroad, they jumped out into the middle of the tracks and linked arms. They stood there, three abreast, facing down a roaring freight train! This was way worse than the M&M machine gun.

When I started yelling for them to get out of the way, one of them said, "No, this is our other game. We do it all the time. Whoever jumps off first loses!"

I thought, *I think whoever jumps off LAST will be the loser!*

Then from behind us, I heard a voice yell, "Todd, Spencer, Jerry! Get off that wailwoad twack!"

The three boys immediately jumped right off the track and scrambled back up the bank.

After we watched the train pass, I turned around to see who had that kind of power. I mean even the school principal couldn't do anything with these boys. There stood Ol' Rayburn. Everybody knew Ol' Rayburn. He lived in a ramshackle house at the far end of the trailer park. Rayburn was mentally retarded. (That's what people called it back then. Now we say "special needs.") He was just kind of always around. Everybody looked out for Ol' Rayburn, and Ol' Rayburn looked out for Todd, Spencer, and Jerry. To be honest, I was a little afraid of Ol' Rayburn, but they weren't. They loved him. He'd give them piggyback rides and tell them the occasional dirty joke. They were as good as blood brothers. If anybody could save those boys from themselves, Rayburn was the one who could do it. When he yelled, "Get off that wailwoad twack!" they obediently jumped right off. There was a mutual respect.

They introduced me. "Hey, Rayburn, this is our friend Tim. He's the preacher's boy."

Now, Rayburn had a certain way. Whenever he greeted someone he would always say, "Hey, Ol' Boy!" Unless you happened to be female. Then he would say, "Hey, Ol' Boy ... Girl!" Because of a crooked leg, he walked with a very pronounced limp. Hobbling around and sticking out a hand to shake mine, Rayburn gave me his traditional greeting. "Hey, Ol'Boy!" And then he followed up with the other thing he always said: "What kind of gun you got?"

That was what he always said, "Hey Ol' Boy! What kind of gun you got?" And before you could answer, he would add, "I got a twenty-two and it'll bwow you head off!"

He didn't have a .22, and he wasn't going to blow anybody's head off. That was just Rayburn's way and everybody knew it. After he got past that little formality, he would talk to you about anything you wanted to talk about. That day he wasn't particularly interested in how I might respond, he just turned and hobbled off across the field and down the lane back to his house before I could say anything.

Todd, Spencer, and Jerry looked at me and one of them asked, "You want to ride bikes?"

I explained I couldn't balance a bike very well, I was still learning.

Todd said, "That's all right. You can ride on the back of my bike. I have a banana seat."

We ran back to their trailer and they pulled out their bicycles from under the front porch. Spencer got on his bike, and Jerry got on his bike with that camera still swinging by the strap around his neck. Todd stood on the pedals of his bike, and I climbed on the banana seat behind him, sitting way back against the sissy bar. We took off down the lane as best we could, but it was difficult with Todd trying to balance both of us.

As we wobbled along he asked, "You wanna learn to ride a bike? You want to learn how to balance? I can learn you. I can learn you real fast!"

We made our way down to the end of the trailer park, and before I knew it, we were in front of Ol' Rayburn's house. I don't think it had ever been painted. The whole structure leaned several degrees to the east. Its tin roof rolled up in several places like the lid of a sardine can. Rayburn was sitting on the front porch rocking back and forth on a rusty, old-fashioned glider.

The three boys wheeled their bicycles around and parked in the lane right in front of Rayburn's gate. Then Todd jumped off his bicycle and climbed on the back of Spencer's, leaving me with the bike all by myself. He hollers across the fence, "Hey Rayburn! Remember this here boy, Tim? The preacher's boy?"

Rayburn obviously remembered. We had just met a few minutes earlier. He gave me his traditional greeting. "Hey Ol' Boy! What kind of gun you got? I got a twenty-two and it'll bwow you head off!"

Before I had time to respond Todd said, "He don't know how to ride a bike and he wants to learn the fast way."

That's when I saw the biggest German Shepherd I have ever seen in my life stand up from the other end of the porch and come dragging a chain like you could pull logs with across the floorboards. It walked to the very edge of the porch steps and pulled its lips back to show white-fanged teeth. I was immediately convinced Rayburn never fed that dog anything but raw meat and unsuspecting social workers. Rayburn jumped up from the glider, grabbed the dog by the collar, unclipped the chain, and yelled, "You go Preacher Boy!"

That beast was off the porch and over the fence in a flash. I took off on the bicycle with that thing snarling behind me like a demon from an exorcism. And under those most unorthodox circumstances, I witnessed my first miracle—I learned how to ride a bicycle instantaneously.

Todd, Spencer, and Jerry had torn off down the lane ahead of me and were yelling over their shoulders, "Go! Go! Go!"

I yelled back, "Ahhh! I'm gonna die! I'm gonna die!"

Suddenly the three boys slid to a stop, and I crashed into them. As we fell into a jumble of wheels, spokes, and sprocket chains, I looked back to see the dog snarl one last warning, turn around, and trot back to the front porch of Ol' Rayburn's house. Rayburn was standing on the top step clapping his hands.

I was still laying among the wreckage when Jerry stood up and waved a still damp, freshly printed Polaroid in the night air. "I got a picture of it."

It was very blurry, but it was documentation that I had learned to ride a bike. I think when you join Hells Angels you have to get a tattoo, but I had a Polaroid picture to prove I had crossed over to perdition!

When we got back to the trailer, my dad was waiting for me. "Their mama says they can come to Sunday School. They're going to start this week."

I thought to myself, *Oh, this is going to be good!*

☆☆☆

The theme for our Sunday School that year was compassion. Each week the teacher told us a story about the compassion of Jesus, sometimes illustrated with flannel graph. Then we went home to look up a Bible verse related to what we had learned. If you returned the next week able to recite your chosen Bible verse from memory, you got a gold star on the chart. For us regular Sunday School kids, flannel graph and memory verses were just the same old, same old. But Todd, Spencer, and Jerry were absolutely captivated. They had never heard any of these stories and soaked them all in.

The first story was very familiar, "The Resurrection of Jairus' Daughter." I had heard it a thousand times. Jairus had a little daughter. She got sick. She died. Jesus came, but he got there too late. The people said, "She's already dead." But Jesus said, "No, she sleeps." And they laughed. They laughed at that family's last hope. But Jesus didn't pay any attention to their laughter. He just went into the sick room, took the little girl by the hand, and said, "Sweetheart, sit up." And she sat right up. (He who laughs last laughs best.)

The next Sunday I stood up and quoted, "And of some have compassion, making a difference. The Book of Jude, verse twenty-two." I did not say "Jude, chapter one, verse twenty-two" because if you've grown up the preacher's kid, you know Jude only has one chapter. You simply say "Jude, verse twenty-two." And of course, I received a gold star to add to my perfect constellation.

Todd, Spencer, and Jerry didn't know about the Book of Jude being a single chapter. I don't think they knew about any chapter from any book of the Bible, but they wanted to earn a gold star. Instead of reciting a Bible verse, Jerry pulled a Polaroid from his back pocket and showed it to the teacher. "See this dead squirrel right here? I felt sorry for it."

We later learned the whole story. Inspired by the resurrection of Jairus' daughter, those boys had gone home to employ a car battery and some jumper cables in a righteous effort to make that squirrel rise again. When it didn't work, they had taken a picture of it and were hoping that would be good enough for a gold star.

The teacher glanced at the photograph with a horrified expression and said, "I'm sorry boys, but I need a Bible verse."

Well, after listening to the rest of us quote verses they realized Bible passages were supposed to be inspirational. So Spencer jumped up, made the Vulcan sign from *Star Trek* and said, "Live long and prosper!"

The teacher shook her head. "That's not in the Bible."

And those three boys, speaking as a chorus, shot back, "But it should be!"

The next story was "Jesus Feeds the Five Thousand." You know that one. Five thousand men, plus women and children, had been listening to Jesus teach all afternoon, and it got to be dinner time. Jesus said to his disciples, "Feed them." The disciples replied, "We don't have anything!" However, there was a little boy who had five loaves and two fish. Jesus broke that into enough food to feed all those people. It was a wonderful miracle.

The next morning the people came back to Jesus and they wanted to be fed again. But he said, "No, I'm not going to keep feeding you, because that was a physical symbol for a spiritual truth. I am the Bread of Life. You must feast on me." And all the people went away, because they didn't understand. (If you don't understand the spiritual application, the story of Jesus feeding the five thousand is like eating Chinese food. You're going to be hungry an hour later.)

The following Sunday I had my Bible verse: "And Jesus went forth and saw a great multitude, and was moved with compassion toward them. Matthew, chapter fourteen, verse fourteen."

As I was pasting another gold star onto the chart Todd, Spencer, and Jerry jumped up from their chairs and sang out "Two all beef patties, special sauce, lettuce, cheese, pickles, onions on a sesame seed bun!"

The teacher smiled. "Boys, that McDonald's Big Mac commercial is not in the Bible."

"But it should be!"

The third story was "Jesus Heals the Paralytic." The house was crowded. There was a crippled man who could not get to the Lord. His friends carried his mat up onto the roof, opened the tiles, and lowered him down to see Jesus. In the midst of that crowd, Jesus looked at this poor crippled man, and said, "Your sins are forgiven you." All the self-righteous Pharisees were shocked! So Jesus asked them, "What's easier? To tell this man that his sins are forgiven, or that he can take up his bed and walk?" Then, he turned back to the crippled man and said, "Take up your bed and walk." The man rolled up his bed and walked right out the door. (And the Pharisees went through the roof!)

After that, Todd, Spencer, and Jerry didn't even try to make up any more Bible verses. When they learned Jesus could heal somebody who could not walk, they brought their friend Ol' Rayburn to Sunday School. Rayburn was not miraculously healed of his crippled leg, but it turned out he loved Sunday School, and came on the church bus with those three boys every week.

Nobody knew what to do with Todd, Spencer, and Jerry, but somebody had a good idea for Rayburn. One of the ushers asked him if he would like to help take up the offering during the worship services. Rayburn loved having a job to do and it turned out to be a really good thing, because if he saw you weren't putting money in the plate, he'd lean over and say, "I got a twenty-two and it'll bwow you head off."

Never again did we have to worry about the offering totals not showing a year-over-year increase. The money just came rolling in. We took on additional missionary projects because of Ol' Rayburn.

✵✵✵

Finally, we came to the end of the Sunday School year and it was time for our annual field trip. We always went to the county fair. Now, you might be wondering, why the county fair? Wouldn't a children's Sunday School class visit a Bible museum or something? No, no, the county fair was a good place for a Sunday School field trip because you could eat your way through the denominations.

Every church in town sponsored a booth selling food related to the culture of their particular congregation. The Catholics were mostly Polish immigrants, so they sold kielbasa with grilled onions stuffed in a big roll with a generous shot of brown mustard. After kielbasa and onions, you'd go to the Baptist Church for fried pie. It's a sin to say so, but I should tell the truth and shame the devil. You can keep the five loaves and two fish whenever I can get a fried pineapple pie! Of course, the Methodists always had fried chicken, and after that you would go to the Pentecostals. They had peanut butter roll. Peanut butter roll is the best stuff ever, like manna from heaven! How to describe it? Well, it's kind of like a white stiff cream over a layer of sweet peanut butter rolled up and sliced like a sweet roll, only it's not a bread, it's a candy. There is nothing better than peanut butter roll that's been patted out by the pious hands of a Pentecostal woman! Last, if you were of age, you could finish off at the Episcopal Church. They ran a moonshine still for historic demonstration purposes.

After eating your way through the denominations, you had two choices: the horse show or the carnival midway. As the preacher's kid, I was never allowed to go near the midway. There were people with multiple piercings and tattoos. It just smacked of the superfluity of heathen naughtiness! But I was allowed to go and see the horse show because it was sponsored by the local Shrine Club.

The Shriners sponsored the whole fair, actually, but the horse show was the main attraction. This was Kentucky, and everybody loved horses. The Shriners used the county fair and horse show as a major fundraiser for their charity, the Crippled Children's Hospital. Nowadays, I think they just call it Children's Hospital, but in those days, it was the Crippled Children's Hospital. You always knew when it was fair time because you would see the familiar posters around town. A picture of a Shriner with his little upside-down flower pot on his head, holding a little boy in leg braces with a crutch, not unlike Bob Cratchit and Tiny Tim. The slogan at the bottom of the poster read "No man ever stood as tall as when he stooped to help a crippled child." Whenever you saw the Crippled Children's Hospital posters you knew it was fair time.

Todd, Spencer, Jerry, and I ran over to the horse ring to discover just one Tennessee Walker trotting round and round all by itself. We thought that was odd. Everybody came to the horse show. They even had a costume class where you didn't have to have a purebred horse. You could just bring your farm pony, let the kids ride around the ring dressed up like Buffalo Bill or Annie Oakley or whatever, and compete for best costume. But none of the ponies were there, just that one Tennessee Walker going round and round. We didn't understand until we heard one of the Shriners say, "The durn Department of Agriculture showed up!" Eventually, we learned what had happened. Whenever there was a horse show, a representative from the Kentucky Department of Agriculture would come from Frankfort to serve as the judge. If you got a judge that was a real stickler for the rules, he would ask each entrant to present immunization papers for their horse to prove they had taken it to a certified equine vet and had it inoculated against communicable diseases.

This particular year the Department of Ag was spot-checking for this thing called Coggins Disease. Now, if you know anything about horses, you've heard of this disease. It is highly contagious, and at that time it seemed to be very prevalent in breeding programs. They thought it was an equine venereal disease. Turns out that's not true, but that's what they thought at the time. They didn't want equine venereal disease going around the horse show, so the judge was checking for negative Coggins papers. He turned away I don't know how many farm trucks pulling horse trailers when they couldn't present the proper paperwork. Barrel-racing quarter horses, show jumpers, and farm kids' ponies were all disqualified. It looked like there would be no horse show at all, but Todd, Spencer, and Jerry saw an opportunity.

Todd said, "Ooh, people are going to be real mad. Let's go over to the farmers' entrance, sit on the gate, and listen to everybody cuss."

We ran across the field and sat on the gate by the road. Farm trucks pulling horse trailers would pull up and the Department of Agriculture would step forward and ask in an official tone, "Can you present negative Coggins papers? We're not admitting any animals without proper documentation."

I learned a vocabulary that is not in the Bible, I can tell you that!

After we had listened to cussing for about a half hour, we heard a familiar voice say, "Hey Ol' Boy!" We looked up to see a farm truck pulling up to the gate with Ol' Rayburn sitting in the passenger seat and calling to us through the rolled-down window. He was wearing a cowboy hat and a vest fashioned out of a brown paper sack with a sheriff's badge drawn with yellow magic marker.

We all jumped off the gate and ran over. "Hey, Rayburn, how are you?"

We learned a local farmer had told Rayburn he could come along with the kids and lead their pony as a cowboy in the costume class. He was all excited about that.

When Rayburn's turn came, the Department of Agriculture stepped up and said, "Can you present negative Coggins papers?"

Rayburn greeted the judge in his usual way. "Hey Ol' Boy! What kinda gun you got?"

The judge ignored the question and continued. "We're not admitting any animals without proper documentation."

Well, Rayburn wasn't finished with his traditional greeting, so he added, "I got a twenty-two and it'll bwow you head off!"

Uh oh!

The judge had been cussed out once too often, and when someone seemingly threatened him with a gun, he called for security. The local sheriff's deputies tried to explain, but it was no good. They ended up escorting Rayburn, the farmer, those children, and that pony off the fairgrounds.

Todd, Spencer, and Jerry went red in the face and headed straight for the carnival midway. I shared their righteous anger, so I threw caution to the wind and joined my friends on that Avenue of Iniquity.

Y'all! I saw things you were never going to experience at Sunday School. There was this game called "The Wheel of Fortune." A big painted wheel with color swatches coming out from the center was laid on a table. At the end of each color swatch was a hole. Pitched next to the table with the wheel was a little striped tent. When a fanfare blared over the loudspeaker, some lights started to swirl around and a woman stepped out of the tent. She was wearing a spangly costume and ripped fishnet stockings. In one hand she carried a big, white lab rat with its pink tail all twisted around her forearm. Walking over to the Wheel of Fortune, she called out, "Place your bets, boys. Place your bets!"

Men quickly crowded around the wheel and started slapping five-dollar bills down on the color swatches, which must have had some sort of light adhesive on them because the bills stuck. Then the woman set the rat in the middle of the wheel and laid a stainless steel bowl over top of it. She spun the wheel round and round and round and round. Then she stopped the wheel and lifted the bowl. The lab rat, all drunk from the spinning, went wobbling out across the wheel, fell down one of those holes, and everybody cheered. The deal was if you had bet on the hole the rat fell through, you won half the pot. This was highly illegal, but it was for the Crippled Children's Hospital. So, nobody complained.

I was standing there fascinated when Todd elbowed me in the ribs and said, "Look over there."

Across the way, there was a tent with a show featuring go-go girls! A prominently displayed sign said you had to be eighteen years of age to be admitted, so we didn't even try. We just stood outside and watched as men would tire of the rat, abandon the Wheel of Fortune, and saunter off toward the go-go girls tent. As we watched, we saw the judge from the Department of Agriculture go into that tent.

I asked my friends, "Why is he going in there? There aren't any horses in that tent."

Spencer said, "He's probably checking for venereal disease."

I honestly don't know if Todd, Spencer, and Jerry had anything to do with what happened next or not. All I know is I went to get some popcorn. While I was gone, somehow or other that rat from the Wheel of Fortune escaped and ran across the stage of the go-go girls tent. There were screams, tent flaps flew up, and scantily clad women went running every which way. The horse judge from the Department of Agriculture was caught in a compromising situation with a floozy from New Jersey, which Jerry documented with his Polaroid camera.

As soon as the film had dried he announced, "Now we're going to have a horse show!"

I said, "How are we going to have a horse show? There's only one horse. We've already seen it."

"No, there's going to be lots of horses now."

We went back over to the horse ring, where that one Tennessee Walker was still trotting round and round. The judge was standing on the lawn in the middle of the ring talking to a couple Shriners. Jerry leaned over the railing, waved that Polaroid overhead, and started yelling, "Hey, Judge! Lookie here, Judge! You missed this one over here. Take a second look, Judge!"

The judge turned around and caught sight of those boys and that picture they were proudly displaying. He whirled back around and held a quick conference with the Shriners. Next thing you know, they announced over the loudspeaker that the Kentucky Department of Agriculture no longer required the presentation of negative Coggins papers. Anybody who wanted to support the Crippled Children's Hospital could bring their horse in and show it at the county fair. A whole bunch of vehicles parked along the highway outside the fairgrounds started up. A parade of trucks and trailers came rolling through the gate to the sound of honking horns, laughing children, and neighing horses.

We watched Ol' Rayburn limp around the show ring, leading a pony while wearing his cowboy hat and paper vest, smiling from ear to ear. He got to be a cowboy after all. Spencer reached up to a telephone pole and yanked off the poster tacked there. As he rolled it up under his arm, he said, "We got our Bible verse!"

We went back to Sunday School the following week. When the teacher asked, "Do you boys have a Bible verse?" Todd, Spencer, and Jerry jumped up, proudly unfurled that poster, and spoke as a chorus, "No man ever stood as tall as when he stooped to help a crippled child!"

The teacher said, "That's not in the Bible."

But she had not witnessed what I had seen, which was nothing short of a genuine act of Christian charity. So I ruined my perfect constellation as I handed my gold star to my friends and said, "But it ought to be!"

THE MANGER SCENE

Wrapped in heavy brown paper with a generic mailing label pasted on one side, other people might have mistaken the package for just another piece of third-class junk mail, but my sister and I were always excited to discover in our mailbox the much anticipated and highly celebrated Sears and Roebuck Christmas Wish Book. The annual catalog would arrive in early fall, but my mother always placed it on a high shelf, well out of our reach, forbidding us to look at it until the afternoon of Thanksgiving Day.

Thanksgiving was always a great event at our house. The cooking started very early in the morning. My sister and I would wake up to the aroma of frying bacon, sautéed onion, and sage from my mother's stuffing mixed with the smell of warm yeast from my dad's rising bread dough. For breakfast, we would get an early taste of the mid-day feast in the form of a hot dinner roll, fresh from the oven and slathered with homemade pumpkin or apple butter. Maybe two rolls, one with each. To keep from messing up our nice dinner clothes, Mom didn't make us get dressed right away. Instead, she would shoo us out of the kitchen to spend the entire morning in our pajamas in front of the television, watching two full hours of pageantry as the world-famous Radio City Music Hall Rockettes literally kicked off the Macy's Thanksgiving Day Parade filled with festive floats, marching bands, and giant balloons. We always watched all the way to the end to see the arrival of Santa Claus!

After the parade, my sister and I would return to the kitchen to inquire about dinner, but, as usual, the little plastic thermometer hadn't popped up from the turkey's breast to indicate it was time for it to come out of the oven. My mother would give us another dinner roll and send us away with the traditional, but nonetheless false, promise, "Dinner will be ready soon. Go play!"

And what did we play? Well, Macy's Thanksgiving Day Parade, of course! My sister would sit on the couch wearing her pajamas, hat, gloves, and scarf. With a big blanket spread over her lap, she would wave to imaginary spectators standing on the curb as she rode down the streets of New York City on a fancy float. With the black Darth Vader cape from my Halloween costume tied around my neck, I would strut around the living room leading my pretend marching band with a broomstick baton.

Eventually, we would both tire of playing parade and wander back into the kitchen. My mother would stuff another dinner roll into our mouths and say, "It won't be long now. Go get dressed in the clothes I've laid out on your beds." We would dress in a hurry, but it didn't make any difference. The turkey wouldn't be ready until it was ready, but our mom was unwilling to allow any more dinner rolls, lest we spoil our appetites. Instead, she would take down the Christmas Wish Book she had been saving for such a time as this.

My sister and I would sit side by side on the couch flipping through every page of the holiday catalog, deeply engaged in our annual tradition of "want that, want that, want that, don't want that." Finally, after what seemed like an eternity, it would be time to eat. As we picked over servings of turkey, dressing, green beans, and mashed potatoes—too full of dinner rolls to really eat all that much—we would chatter away about everything we wanted for Christmas from the pages of the Sears and Roebuck Christmas Wish Book.

After the Thanksgiving feast my dad would always say, "Let's take a nap and give our food time to settle before we have a slice of pumpkin pie with a cup of coffee."

Anticipating our unwillingness to sleep, my mother employed one of her best parenting tricks. Opening a kitchen drawer, she would take out a black magic marker, hand it to us, and say, "While your father and I are napping, you may each circle three things you want for Christmas." Then, she would remind us, "Choose carefully, because that magic marker is permanent."

Our deliberations kept us occupied for a long time, allowing my parents to have some well-deserved peace and quiet. It also allowed our mother to call in the order the following day on Black Friday, knowing the shipment would arrive before Christmas.

As children, it never occurred to us our parents also enjoyed paging through the Wish Book until my sister and I discovered our mom sitting on the couch studying the Christmas catalog with a big magnifying glass one year. Our mother was born with very poor vision, and the small print on the slick, shiny pages was nearly impossible for her to read. However, with the help of her magnifying glass she was admiring the pictures in a two-page spread showcasing different types of manger scenes. She particularly liked a set of painted porcelain figurines from Germany. There was also a beautiful crystal set from Czechoslovakia and another hand-carved from olive wood imported from the Holy Land.

We already had a manger scene made of plastic. The Holy Family, plus two shepherds, three wise men, a few sheep, and a camel, always sat atop a bookcase my dad wrapped with heavy, brick-patterned, corrugated paper to make it look like a fireplace for Christmas. The four-inch figures were pretty, but my mom couldn't see them very well. Noting that all the manger scenes in the catalog were much larger, she sighed, "I wish we could afford one of these big ones so that I could really see it."

✼✼✼

A few days later, we went to Mack's, the local grocery store. My sister and I loved that store, because in the back of Mack's Grocery there was a Ben Franklin Five and Dime stocked with all kinds of junk for kids to look at while their parents shopped for groceries. You could plunder through shelves filled with games, tools, squirt guns, bean bag furniture, plastic lawn ornaments, books, and bags of potting soil. At Christmastime there would be special displays with all kinds of trinkets and toys for stocking stuffers. After our parents got a buggy and started their grocery shopping, my sister and I ran to the back to see what seasonal treasures we might find. Rounding an end cap at the top of the first aisle, we discovered the biggest Joseph, Mary, and Baby Jesus we had ever seen. Molded in hard plastic, each figure stood three feet tall and came fitted with an interior light bulb, allowing the tableau of the Holy Family to be beautifully illuminated from within.

My sister spoke first. "Mommy could see that!"

I checked the price tag. As I remember, the three figures and the plastic manger cost sixty dollars plus tax. But it might as well have been six thousand plus tax, because we didn't have that kind of money.

My sister said, "We don't have to have all the money today. We can put it on layaway."

She pulled Mary down from the shelf, and I grabbed Joseph, the baby, and the plastic manger. We hurried to the service counter at the very back of the store where we met a nice lady wearing a pair of sparkly magnifying glasses on a chain around her neck.

As we struggled to hoist the figures up onto the counter she asked, "Well, now what do we have here?"

I breathlessly explained, "We want to put this on lay-away as a Christmas present."

"It's going to be a surprise for our mom," my sister added.

"Certainly," said the layaway lady. "I'll make sure to keep your secret. Let's just look at the price." She slipped on her magnifiers to see the handwritten tag. Tapping the keys on an adding machine, she said, "You'll need a down payment equal to twenty percent of the total plus tax, which is sixty-three fifty-five."

I fished into my pockets and my sister rummaged around in her little purse. We placed some wrinkled bills and loose change on the counter. The layaway lady very patiently straightened the bills and counted the coins. Finally, she said, "You have a total of four dollars and eighty-nine cents, which is exactly what you need."

We stood there grinning all over ourselves as she wrote the amount of our down payment onto her receipt pad and explained that layaway payments on holiday items could be made any time until four on Christmas Eve.

Our goal would require sacrifice and determination, and we were starting with less than the required down payment, but the layaway lady at the Ben Franklin Five and Dime did us a great favor by not discounting that manger scene one red cent. We would appreciate it more by having to earn every penny. Even before leaving the store, we were already plotting and planning schemes to raise the required funds in the short time before Christmas. We both agreed to contribute the full amounts of our weekly allowances toward the cause. Realizing that wouldn't be enough, my sister decided to skip lunch every day at school. I loved my momma, but I didn't want to skip lunch.

One of my regular chores was to do the milking. We didn't have a big farm, just a single goat. My dad cared for a milk goat when he was a kid and was convinced it built character, so he insisted I care for a milk goat, too. Every morning before daylight and every evening before dark, I performed the same set of tasks. To this day, I can go through the motions of measuring out goat chow, pouring it into the feedbox, washing the goat's udder with a clean cloth, squeezing the milk into a sterilized pail, carrying the pail to the kitchen, pouring it through a strainer, storing the milk in the refrigerator, and finally washing the milk pail so it was ready for the next time. This twice-daily ritual, predictable as the rising and the setting of the eternal sun, never varied, except for one cold December evening when I poured the goat chow into the feedbox only to be startled by a huge rat jumping out of the trough and scurrying across the floor to escape through a hole at the bottom of the barn wall.

Thankful the rat simply ran away, I continued with my chore. But as I sat on the milking stool, I kept seeing the rodent's image in my mind. The disgusting thing must have been a foot and a half long, and it moved with a loathsome, slithering motion that made me shudder all over. Suddenly, I was struck with the reality of what I had seen. I was sitting in a cold, dark, milking shed with a goat eating from a trough, very much like the manger where the infant Jesus had slept. He had not been born into a beautiful arrangement of sparkling crystal or exquisitely painted figurines. The first manger scene took place in a real barn just like mine, occupied by sheep and goats just like mine, and with rats and vermin just like mine. The real Nativity was a pitiful scene of utter humility into which The King of Glory voluntarily entered out of eternal love for boys just like me.

As I finished milking the goat, hot tears trickled down my cheeks. I was still thankful the rat had run away, but I was even more thankful for having seen it in the first place. Before I left the barn, I had decided to join my sister in skipping a few school lunches and contributing the money to our Christmas surprise.

For nearly a month we scraped, skimped, begged, and borrowed. We didn't tell our parents anything, but they grew suspicious when we repeatedly asked to go shopping at Mack's Grocery. Little by little we had managed to reduce the total debt down to nine dollars and forty-two cents. The desperately needed funds arrived by mail the day before Christmas Eve in the form of two five-dollar bills tucked into holiday cards from our grandparents. With the money in hand, we started begging our parents to take us back to the store one last time. My dad said, "I wasn't planning on making another trip to town this week, but since it's Christmas Adam ..."

(You may not be familiar with our family tradition of Christmas Adam. That's what we always called the day before Christmas Eve. Get it? Never mind, I don't have time to explain. We have a manger scene to purchase!)

Making Mom and Dad promise to stay in the car, my sister and I ran with our five-dollar bills to the back of the store. Our friend, the layaway lady with the sparkly glasses on a chain, congratulated us by saying, "I hoped that you could do it, but I was a little worried since tomorrow is Christmas Eve."

Moments later my sister and I came out lugging a huge box wrapped in plain brown paper. We were so excited we couldn't wait for our dad to drive us home. We stuffed the box into the back seat, climbed in on either side, and exclaimed, "Mom! This surprise is for you! Open it now!"

Our mother looked at our father. "Did you help with this?"

My father raised a hand as if swearing to tell the truth in a court of law. "Not one bit."

"Open it now! Open it now!"

Mom reached back and grabbed a corner of the brown paper, tearing it away to reveal the label on the side of the box picturing a thirty-six-inch Joseph, a thirty-two-inch Mary, and a thirteen-inch Baby Jesus in a plastic manger.

"And it lights up!" we immediately informed her.

Smiling through tears, my mom said, "Well then, I will have no trouble seeing that."

We drove home to set up the manger scene under the plum tree in the front yard. By the time Dad ran the extension cord from the house it was already getting dark. As we stood admiring the beautifully illuminated figures, I kept asking my mom over and over, "Do you like it, Mom? Do you really like it?" She assured me she did and reminded me I still needed to feed the goat and do the evening's milking. I think she really did like her surprise, because she was still standing in the front yard looking at the manger scene when I returned from the barn. She declared then and there that we had started a new family tradition: Every year, on Christmas Adam, we would place the big plastic figures in the front yard and light them up as soon as it got dark.

That tradition has continued for more than forty years. The original figures of Joseph, Mary, and Baby Jesus are set up in my parents' front yard every year the day before Christmas Eve. Over the decades the plastic figures faded, and a few years ago my dad repainted them. Now Joseph's robe is no longer red, but more of a pukey purple and Mary's skin tone is so dark she looks like a poster girl for the local tanning salon. Baby Jesus looks okay, but there's a short in his lightbulb. So, for a few moments he is the Light of the World. Then he is not. Then he's the Light of the World again. Then he's not. My sister and I have offered to replace the manger scene with a new one, but Mom will have no other. It is her favorite Christmas decoration. I suppose that's understandable. The old, faded figures have special meaning for her and my dad, and my sister and me. I hope they also have special meaning for anyone else who might drive past my parents' house. I pray they will be reminded that Jesus came to Earth so those of us who were blind might see.

BEING
SOUTHERN

SMOKY AND STINKY

Before my storytelling career took off, I worked as a carriage-driving tour guide for more than two years and had many great adventures. I often reminisce about those days with nostalgic affection, and people say, "You really seem to have enjoyed that work. Do you ever miss it?"

My most frequent reply? "I miss my horse."

As a tour guide, you work with lots of people, all kinds of people. There are the tourists, of course, who come to Charleston from everywhere (even unimaginable places like New Jersey), but they all have one thing in common. They have come to Charleston, the city where history lives, to see two-hundred-year-old homes filled with priceless antiques, designer fabrics, and expensive art. Standing in stark contrast to the tourists are the owners of these historic homes, who love the prestige of living in a two-hundred-year-old mansion furnished with priceless antiques, designer fabrics, and expensive art; but they don't want anybody to look at them.

The tour guide's job is to keep both groups happy as you roll through the streets in a horse-drawn carriage, telling stories from the land of sweet tea and slavery. It is not an easy balance. No matter what you do, someone is bound to be offended. That's why I say from my carriage driving days, I miss my horse. His name was Ben. He was a big, blonde Belgian with a slow walk, an easy-going personality, and he never took offense at anything I said. I miss Ben ... and Smoky and Stinky.

Now, Smoky and Stinky weren't horses, they were men. They were men of a particular and rare breed. They were Gullah men. Of course, as you already know, Gullah is the centuries-old culture of enslaved West Africans and their descendants living along the South Carolina coast. Most often when you hear a tour guide use the term Gullah, they are referring to the Gullah creole language. Since I'm telling a story about my carriage-driving days, let me give you a little sample by translating an old nursery rhyme about a horse and rider.

> *Yankee Doodle went to town riding on a pony.*
>> *Dat bye done make skrate fuh town pontop a horse what ain't no biggah den fuh keep 'em fuh drag e' foots.*
> *Stuck a feather in his hat and called it macaroni.*
>> *'E done put duh turkrey cock fedduh in 'e hat pontop 'e head and now 'e tink e' duh been bohn duh high Buckruh.*

Being native to the Gullah culture and speaking this creole language is distinctive, but that's not what made these two barn hands completely and utterly original. Not only were Smoky and Stinky Gullah by birth, but they possessed a unique perspective on the world and dispensed a lifetime of gathered wisdom in pithy, proverbial form as they mucked stalls, fed and curried the animals, and pitched hay. They were marvelous examples of the human race. Of all the people I worked with during my carriage-driving days—tourist, native, highbrow and low-born—these two were my favorites. As they say in the Gullah language, "Dey ben gentmun fuh true!"

My first day on the job, the owner of the carriage company introduced me by simply saying "This here is Smoky and Stinky. They can tell you everything you need to know."

Well, the first thing I needed to know was how to hitch a horse. My first lesson went kind of like this. Stinky looks at me and says, "A'ight! Duh fus' 'ting whatsonebuh yuh gwine do is fuh to futch do collah from de peg long duh wall. All deh horse got e own peg wid deh name set down pontop a board obuh dey peg. Take 'em and wrap it round ol' Ben neck and latch dem two ting pon deh top deh."

I just stood there.

It was immediately apparent I had no idea what had just been said to me. So, Smoky steps over to a big rack along the wall and takes down a horse collar hanging from a peg. I noticed my horse's name, Ben, hand-printed on a board tacked to the wall above the peg. He slips the collar up around the horse's neck, buckles two latches at the top, then steps back and makes a little gesture as if to say "ta-da." Then he unbuckled the collar and removed it from the horse's neck. He handed it to me and without saying a word, gave me a look that said, "OK, your turn."

I stepped up to the horse and slipped the collar around his neck and fastened the two buckles at the top. When I finished I didn't know what to say, so I stepped back and made a little gesture as if to say, "ta-da." Smoky and Stinky looked at one another and said, "A'ight!" Then they proceeded with the lesson. Stinky gave me instructions in Gullah. I stood there like an idiot. Smoky stepped forward and demonstrated. I imitated what he did and they pronounced my work satisfactory with an "A'ight!"

After we had finished hitching the horse, Stinky pointed to the collar, the very first piece of equipment they demonstrated, and said, "Ain't nebbuh spose tuh lif' 'em obuh 'e head 'cause dish yuh horse ain't like dat ting fuh tetch e' yeah. If'n dat ting tech e' yeah den e gwine stomp. An' if'n 'e come down pontop yuh foot, e crack e bone."

By his tone of voice I knew this final bit of instruction was very important, but I had no idea what it was. So, Smoky pantomimed placing a pre-buckled collar over the horse's head. As he did so, he purposely tickled Ben's ear. The horse immediately stomped his big foot. Smoky jumped back, grabbed his toe, and began hopping around while he made a little yelp as if he were suffering terrible pain.

I am not as good a storyteller as Smoky was pantomimist, because it is impossible for me to explain just how effectively this brief drama communicated that my horse had a nervous tick. If I made the mistake of slipping the collar pre-buckled over the horse's head and bumped his ears, then he would stomp and I would be in danger of him breaking a bone in my foot. It was best to slide the collar up from beneath and buckle it into place to avoid touching his sensitive ears.

That's pretty much how I learned to hitch a horse. I could teach you if you're good at charades, because that's how I learned.

Now this teaching method worked well enough, but as a person fascinated by language, not to mention being an aspiring folklorist and storyteller, I didn't want to always rely on Smoky's excellent mime skills to understand what Stinky was saying to me. So I hung around the barn as much as possible and listened to these older gentlemen converse with one another. I also went to the library and checked out books on the Gullah language. And I listened to Gullah field recordings at the South Carolina Historical Society. Over the course of a long, hot summer—three or four months I suppose—I began to understand what they were saying. Mostly. Some. A little bit.

At least I eventually learned to identify every part of a horse harness. Stinky took great delight in quizzing me. He would hold up a particular piece and say, "Betcha ain't know what dis yuh is."

And I would say, "Those are the hames. They rest against the collar."

Then he would ask, "Whyfore dush yuh?"

And I would reply, "Those are the traces. They are attached to the hames and run all the way back to the single tree."

Whenever Stinky would quiz me, Smoky was always standing by watching. But his role as silent actor had been eliminated when I learned to understand what Stinky was saying. You could tell he wanted to show his approval, but he wasn't used to being the one who did the talking. Instead, after I had successfully answered one of Stinky's questions, Smoky would raise his eyebrows way up as if he had seen a ghost and just laugh, "Hee hee hee!"

On the day I answered every question correctly, Stinky leaned back and said, "Well, ain't 'e a berry soon man whut done climb den acklowdgement tree! A gentmun fuh true."

I understood this expression as being the Gullah version of how white people say, "You are a gentleman and a scholar."

Smoky agreed with his customary "Hee hee hee!"

One day, Stinky surprised me with a pop quiz. He picked up a loop of leather and said, "What dis?"

I very confidently answered, "That's called the crupper. It loops around the horse's tail, but it's an optional piece and we don't normally put it on." I waited, expecting Smoky to give me his approving laugh.

Instead, he spoke up in regular English. "Loops around its tail? Well, any horse's ass would know that!"

Then they both shot their eyebrows up. "Hee hee hee!"

I had been played! They could speak English any time they wanted, but they chose not to just for my benefit. However, their little ruse communicated to me that if I was willing to be the butt of their jokes, they were willing to let me hang around the barn and learn from them.

Not long after that, I inquired about their names. Smoky's nickname made complete sense. You never saw him without a cigarette in his mouth. But Stinky's was more of a mystery. These men were every bit double my age and then some. And I did not think it was proper to call them by nicknames. I told them my grandmother had taught me to respect my elders, and I should call them by their surnames. If they would please tell me their proper names, I would very much appreciate it.

They looked me up and down and Stinky said, "If'n it mean dat much to you grandmama, den it's MISTER Stinky to you."

And that was that. He would never tell me his proper name.

✳✳✳

I learned to appreciate these men for their perspective and their sense of humor. I don't know how to describe it except to say it was clownish wisdom. However, not everyone appreciated their antics. We had a horse trainer at the carriage company. We'll call him Clyde to protect his true identity, and also because he had formerly worked for the farm in St. Louis, Missouri that raised and trained the Budweiser Clydesdales. Clyde knew everything about horses and their behavior, because he had worked with the Budweiser Clydesdales. He knew the best procedures for the barn, because he had worked with the Budweiser Clydesdales. He knew everything about managing a carriage company, because he had worked with the Budweiser Clydesdales. Clyde knew everything about everything because ... well, you know.

If that wasn't enough to make you sick, Clyde also had the distinct disadvantage of being from "off." That means he wasn't originally from the American South, by a long shot. In Charleston, there are three distinct classes of people. First there are "natives." These are the fortunate few who are born with a full measure of God's grace. Then there are people from "away." That's folks from other parts of the American South who can obtain Divine favor by marrying well. And then there are the people from "off." Now that's not as bad as it might sound. Being from "off" does not preclude one from being able to find a respectable place in Charleston society. However, you must display a large amount of humility and put forth a strenuous effort to overcome this moral deficiency. I never could ascertain whether Clyde was unaware of his shortcomings or if he simply didn't care.

He was in charge at the barn whenever the owner of the carriage company wasn't present, which gave him all the authority he needed to boss Smoky and Stinky around and make their lives miserable. He particularly didn't like how they were all the time cutting up in the barn. They were too loud. He didn't like how slow they moved. They wasted time. He didn't like the way they arranged all the tack hanging on the wall. They seemed to be completely unfamiliar with how it was done for the Budweiser Clydesdales. And whenever he caught Smoky with a cigarette in his mouth, there were always words. Clyde would throw some cuss words at Smoky. Then, Smoky would throw some cuss words right back at Clyde. Of course, Smoky always cussed in Gullah so you couldn't understand anything he was saying. I think he called Clyde a "son of a Budweiser Clydesdale" once, but I'm not certain.

Now I will admit, it is not at all wise to smoke cigarettes in a barn where the floor is littered with dry, combustible hay. However, to Smoky's credit, the cigarette in his mouth was usually unlit. He would only light it if he was standing in the shower stall bathing a horse. If somebody said, "Smoky, you really shouldn't be lighting up in the barn," he would hold up the water hose and respond, "Dey ain't gwine be no fiah. Dish yeh hose pipe dey dey side me."

As you can imagine, Clyde was not satisfied with this explanation.

I tried to help Clyde, since he was from "off" by explaining Smoky and Stinky were not the kind of employees who were going to go to human resources with concerns over a personality conflict. If he didn't let up a little, they were much more likely to hide around the corner of the barn, and when he walked by completely unsuspecting, hit him over the head with a manure shovel. But Clyde just informed me a manure shovel was not the right tool for hitting someone over the head. I washed my hands of it by saying, "I know, I know. You learned a better way to commit murder when you worked with the Budweiser Clydesdales."

One day there was a particularly heated row, and Clyde ended his rant by saying Smoky and Stinky could easily be replaced. But that was not true. You could get different barn help, but there would never be another Smoky and Stinky.

My horse, Ben, was a very calm and predictable fellow. I've never driven another horse I liked better. There were no surprises with Ben, which is the way you want it when navigating busy city streets with an 1800-pound animal. Dealing with the public, on the other hand, was never the same twice. You never knew who was going to climb aboard your carriage or what they might say. On many an occasion, I was left more or less dumbfounded, but Smoky and Stinky always knew exactly how to respond.

One day I had a native-born Charlestonian on my carriage. A genuine, blue-blooded SOB. (The SOB stands for "South of Broad." All the addresses below that historic street are particularly prestigious, and Charlestonians proudly proclaim this fact when introducing themselves to others.) It was highly unusual for a native to do anything touristy in the historic town, and most wouldn't be caught dead on a "buggy ride." But this woman's granddaughter was visiting from out of town and the carriage tour was a treat to amuse the child. When the lady climbed aboard my rig, she spread out a sheet of newspaper to sit on, ensuring her skirt did not make contact with the carriage seat.

After she was settled with her granddaughter but before we left the carriage barn, she peeked up at me from beneath her giant sun hat, looking as if she had just eaten a tourist for breakfast, and asked, "Carriage driving, is this a career path for you?"

I smiled and said, "No, I see this opportunity not so much as a career path but more as a stepping stone." I then briefly explained I had recently graduated with a theater degree and was endeavoring to become a folklorist and professional storyteller.

She shot up an eyebrow and exclaimed, "Storytelling? That can't pay much."

I smiled again. "True, the earnings potential doesn't equal what a doctor or lawyer might expect, but it's my passion. I might not get rich, but it will certainly be interesting."

She did not return my smile. "You ought to try rich. I rather like it."

My smile melted, as I struggled to think of a comeback. I really wanted to say something, but I could tell this lady was very accustomed to having the last word.

It was Smoky, the man of few words, who actually ended the conversation. Just as the old SOB uttered her comment with a grand look of superiority, Smoky gave my horse a little slap on the rump. It was just enough to make Ben slightly startle. He didn't bolt, but he stepped out of the barn with a bit of jerk, which jolted the old lady and caused her to grab hold of her granddaughter and discontinue any further conversation with me. As I rolled out on to the street, I looked back at Smoky. He was standing in the barn door with that unlit cigarette dangling from his lips, shaking his head. He didn't say anything other than "Mmm, mmm, mmm."

I immediately realized this little utterance, "Mmm, mmm, mmm," could be a very useful exclamation when words fail you. I started to notice Smoky and Stinky employed the expression regularly. I also began to understand it could effectively communicate utter condemnation or high approval, depending on the context. "Mmm, mmm, mmm."

Then one day I realized it could express disdain for one thing and praise for another at the very same time.

I had a family climb aboard my carriage with a very active—or more accurately, hyperactive—boy of about seven or eight years of age. He was instantly all over the carriage, which was a big sixteen-passenger surrey with four bench seats seating four people each. Since this was a family of four—father, mother, boy, girl—I asked them to sit all together on one bench, leaving room for others on the remaining seats. Of course, they let little Mr. Jumpy pick, and he chose the very front seat, but couldn't settle on which position.

First he wanted to sit next to his dad. He was no sooner seated then he changed his mind and climbed across his whole family to sit by his mom. And then back again. Every time he clambered over, he would reach out and try to grab the horse's reins out of my hands. I informed him this was not a cowboy movie and he could not slap the horse with the reins yelling "Heeyah!" Upon receiving this news, he flopped down on the very far right edge of the bench seat to sulk. Then I had to request that he sit between his parents in the middle. This was a strict safety policy of the carriage company. There are no seatbelts in a carriage, and if you hit a bump, a child could potentially fall out. The family complied, but let me know they didn't like the policy one bit. Trying to avoid any further conflict, I changed the subject, chatting them up while we waited on other passengers to climb aboard. I asked them what other attractions or historic sites they planned to see while in town.

The father quickly and enthusiastically informed me they were taking the ferry out to the little island in the mouth of the harbor to tour Fort Sumter.

I said, "Oh, that's a great thing to do with kids. Your son is certain to see dolphins playing in the harbor."

"We ain't looking for dolphins. We are visiting to memorialize the Confederate fallen."

"Certainly," I replied. "That is where the American Civil War began."

He corrected me. "There was nothing civil about the War of Northern Aggression."

I kept quiet, but thought, *Oh, he's one of those.*

Then, he informed me that while they were at the fort, his son was going to get himself a Confederate flag. He went on and on about this flag and how his son would proudly display it in his bedroom. I thought, *Not only can he not let it go, but he's raising his own little rebel.*

My thought was interrupted by the boy jumping up and shouting, "If I had it now, I could wave it on this carriage tour!"

Well, I had flags on my carriage, but not the kind they were talking about. These were little orange plastic flags mounted on thin sticks and stuck into old tennis balls. We used them every day ... as horse urine markers. Whenever your horse let loose in the street it left behind gallons of the foul-smelling stuff. We carriage drivers would reach down to the floor of the surrey, take a little orange flag, and throw it into the puddle with a splash. It would bob around in there until Smoky and Stinky were able to come along and clean the street. They called it Pee Patrol, driving around the historic district in a pickup truck outfitted with hoses and a big tank of deodorizing liquid. Whenever they saw a little orange flag, Smoky and Stinky would stop the truck, hop out, spray away the stench, and toss the little flag into the back of the truck. Every morning they would restock each carriage. We used the same flags over and over.

Here I was, once again, at a loss for how to handle these people, but Smoky came to my rescue. He had been standing next to my carriage listening to this entire conversation. Very quietly, he reached into the carriage, took one of those horse urine markers, and lifted it up to the boy's eye level. Then he looked at me and very quietly muttered, "He want a flag. Ain't no reason to wait 'til he get to Fort Sumter."

The boy grabbed that flag and started waving it around. I looked at him and said, "You can keep that as a complimentary souvenir of your carriage tour." Then I clicked at my horse and rolled out of the barn.

As I glanced back at Smoky, he was standing in the barn door with his hand raised to his forehead in a silly salute. I caught his eye and with mutual understanding we uttered in unison that simple, yet meaningful phrase: "Mmm, mmm, mmm!"

☆☆☆

Now I don't want you to get the false impression that every single tour I conducted was filled with hard-to-handle types. I had plenty more trips around the historic city with delightful people from all over the world. One particular young fellow is very memorable because he turned out to be the complete opposite of the little rebel. This young man was about ten years of age and covered in freckles. In his plaid shirt and blue jeans he was the very image of the "all-American boy," a real-life Tom Sawyer. He sat up on the edge of his seat with wide-eyed curiosity and enthusiastically took in the whole tour, asking questions, snapping photos, and thoroughly enjoying himself.

When we got back to the barn after our sixty-minute tour, he stood up and thrust a hand in his pants pocket to extract a shiny quarter as he exclaimed, "That was the best carriage tour I have ever had the privilege to go on and I want to give you this twenty-five cents as a tip!"

Everyone else on the carriage smiled with amusement, as I graciously thanked him for his generosity, pocketed the coin, and shook his hand, man-to-man.

After some photos with the horse, Tom Sawyer and his family walked away, and my tour guide buddies started ragging me. "I can't believe you took that little boy's quarter!" "You robbed that kid of his candy money!" But I could tell by the look on the kid's face that he really wanted to give me a tip, not so much as an act of generosity, but as a way of being all grown up. I was struggling to explain this to my fellow tour guides when Stinky stepped up and put it best by saying, "Y'all hesh up! Tim ben' lak uh dat b'ys saa'bint, so dat b'y could skretch 'eself up fuh mek lak e' ben duh king!" (You all be quiet. Tim bent like a servant so that boy could stand tall and pretend to be a king.)

I was grateful to Stinky for explaining it so eloquently. "Yeah," says I, "Dat be fuh true!"

If you took the time to listen, Smoky and Stinky very often provided spot-on commentary. All of us tour guides had witnessed it time and again. For instance, everybody knew what they called Clyde. And it wasn't "son of a Budweiser Clydesdale." No, they referred to him as a "Cumyah," which was their way of saying Clyde was from "off." In Gullah, there are two groups of people: "Beenyahs" and "Cumyahs." A "beenyah" has "been here" all along, native born. A "cumyah" just "came here" and doesn't understand local customs and traditions. Clyde was definitely a "cumyah," especially when it came to understanding anything spoken in the Gullah language.

Smoky and Stinky used that to their advantage, particularly if Smoky wanted to sneak a cigarette while bathing horses in the shower stall. To protect his friend from the wrath of Clyde, Stinky would stand at the back door of the barn to keep an eye out for the boss. If he saw him coming, Stinky would loudly say, "Mmm, mmm, mmm! Yuh kin hide duh fiah, but wha' cha gwine do widduh smoack!" That is to say, "Uh oh! You can hide the fire, but what are you going to do with the smoke?" Then, Smoky would drop the cigarette down the floor drain of the shower stall and feign complete innocence.

This system worked pretty well until the day Clyde came into the barn from a different direction. Smoky was standing in the shower stall with his back to the door bathing Ben. It was evident he had a lit cigarette in his mouth, because even though his back was turned, you could see a trail of smoke rising up over his head.

Clyde yelled, "Smoky!"

Realizing he was about to be caught, Smoky continued soaping the horse with a sponge in one hand and the water hose in the other. With one quick, silent motion, he opened his mouth, flipped that short stub over, and closed his mouth, snuffing the cigarette with his tongue. It was one of the most amazing maneuvers I have ever seen. No fire-eater at the circus could have done it better. Clyde was not impressed, and a shouting match ensued.

This one was different. The row was completely one-sided. Clyde was doing all the shouting and Smoky wasn't saying a word. He just continued to sponge the horse with one hand and hold the hose in the other. He wouldn't even look at Clyde. I suppose it was hard for Smoky to talk with a snuffed cigarette butt in his mouth. At first I thought *Uh oh! Smoky is extra mad this time. He's letting it build up before he pounds Clyde once and for all.* I considered quietly removing the manure shovel propped in the corner of the shower stall. I should have known Smoky was much more creative than that.

Smoky kept on working as Clyde ranted, but he was moving slower and slower and slower. This passive resistance infuriated Clyde even more. Finally, he stepped forward and snatched the sponge out of Smoky's hand, saying, "Move over! This is taking forever. I'll do it myself!"

Smoky looked Clyde dead in the eye with an absolutely expressionless face as he handed him the hose and sponge and stepped away from the horse. Clyde started furiously scrubbing the horse and Smoky very calmly walked around to the other side of the huge animal where he was completely hidden from view. He silently opened his mouth and let the cigarette butt fall unnoticed down the floor drain. Then, before closing his lips, he stuck his finger into his mouth and swished it around to ensure it was completely covered in spit. Still hidden from Clyde's view, he reached up and stuck his saliva-slicked finger right down into my horse's ear. Ben raised a hoof the size of a frying pan and stomped.

With his foot pinned to the floor under the crushing weight of a draft horse, Clyde was now yelling his head off and flailing against the side of the enormous animal in a desperate attempt to move the 1800-pound beast. Smoky looked at Stinky and they both said, "Mmm, mmm, mmm" as they walked out of the barn.

Over the course of the next two weeks, I witnessed Smoky, and sometimes Stinky, pull that trick again and again. They didn't do it every day, just often enough to keep Clyde dressed in steel-toed boots and completely frustrated he couldn't train that nervous tick out of my horse. Not terribly long after that, Clyde left the employment of our carriage company, but he didn't go back to St. Louis and the Budweiser Clydesdales. No, he went to work for a mule breeder in Tennessee. I could make a joke about how he was probably much better suited to that particular animal's temperament, but I will refrain. However, I will say after he was gone, we tour guides had a little get together with Smoky and Stinky one evening after work. We celebrated with a six pack of ... Pabst Blue Ribbon.

BACK SURGERY

Y'all! I suffered a herniated disc. At first I didn't know I had herniated a disc. All I knew was that over a period of several weeks I had gathered all the necessary elements for a good story. At least that's what I concluded when people would express empathy for my mortal pain by saying, "I'm sorry your back hurts, but at least when you get through this you'll have a good story to tell."

Be honest. Have you ever said something stupid like that? I know you have, so don't try to deny it. Except if you're from the South you didn't say it in those words. What you probably said was, "Well, you know what the Bible says, 'What doesn't kill you only makes you stronger.'"

That's not in the Bible. But if that's the best comfort you can offer a person in obvious agony, then I will share my favorite Biblical quotation with you: "Shut up!"

For too long the source of my suffering was a mystery. When I consulted the doctor he began with the least invasive procedure, which meant he asked me questions about my back and had his billing department charge me an arm and a leg. The doctor wanted to know if I had been in a car accident. I assured him I had never been in a car accident in my life. I am a very good driver, which I attribute to not having learned to drive in Los Angeles or any other manic metropolis. Consequently, speed and recklessness are not factors. Nor do I have any family heritage tracing to New Jersey, so I am not prone to excessive use of the horn. Once, I did incur the consequences of a slight miscalculation of distance when traveling on the freeway in Atlanta, but other than that isolated incident, I have never suffered a serious traffic infraction.

My physician asked me if I had suffered strain as a result of heavy lifting. I boldly informed the good doctor I had not told the truth since the spring of 1987. He failed to see the correlation, requiring me to explain I was a professional storyteller. As such I am nothing more than a bald-faced liar by trade and the moral burden of the occupation is a heavy load on my conscience. As a raconteur I shun all physical labor because I am unable to handle the additional stress. (You may wonder, by comparison, how the related occupations of lawyer and politician hold up under the same weight and strain of untruth. Well, a lawyer has his money and a politician has yours.)

It was speculated that my spinal injury was due to a sudden twist or turn, but this also was an impossibility as I am a man firm in my convictions and not easily persuaded to repent the pleasure of being a liar. To the contrary, I rather enjoy it and would never consider a sudden turn away from the joy of telling tales for a living.

Finally, a battery of medical tests was ordered. After a CAT scan, an MRI, and a mammogram that violated my right to privacy, it was determined I had completely herniated the disc between the fourth and fifth lumbar sections of my spine. This injury was most likely caused by undue exertion from getting ready to do something. Whatever I was getting ready to do has long been completely forgotten. But nonetheless, like most Southerners, I find the mental effort of preparing for physical exertion strenuous enough to cause more than a mild discomfort. Most Southerners express this phenomenon with the classic phrase "I'm fixin' to ...," as in "I'm fixin' to climb up on the roof and saw off that tree limb."

That's exactly what my dad said one afternoon. Whenever the phrase "I'm fixin' to" is uttered by one of the male members of my family, the corresponding female—generally, his wife or mother—begins to secure copious amounts of gauze bandaging and bottles of mercurochrome. My father's utterance of that fateful phrase ended with my mother calling me on the telephone. When I said "hello," she said "We're alright."

I immediately asked why she had begun the conversation with "We're alright."

"Well, after your daddy said 'I'm fixin' to climb up on the roof and saw off that tree limb,' he asked me to hold the ladder. When he fell off the roof he landed on me and I landed on the chainsaw."

I was so horrified at this news that I could only gasp, but my mother reassured me by repeating, "We're alright. I've already seen the doctor for just a few stitches, and if

I apply enough Mary Kay foundation with just the right shade of lipstick you can hardly even tell."

That's the kind of thing that happens when men in my family say "I'm fixin' to." At least that's true on my father's side. On my mother's side, no one has ever been at the slightest risk of injury from fixin' to do anything. As a rule, on that side of the family, bodily harm usually follows the phrase, "Hey, y'all! Watch this!"

But I digress from the main purpose of my discourse, which is to relate to you in vivid and exhaustive detail the great pain and suffering caused by my herniated disc. (This perseveration on one's personal pain and mental distress is what we Southerners refer to as "carrying on a bit.")

For a proper appreciation of this ghastly tale you must be acquainted with the level of my grief, the power of my pain. This was not a minor inconvenience such as you might suffer when your mother-in-law comes to visit. No siree, Bob! The discomfort was nothing short of a lightning strike in my lower back, radiating through my left buttock, wrapping around my left thigh, traveling over my knee and down my shin to shoot across the top of my foot and exit out the end of my big toe. It was horrible. There was no comfortable position. I could not stand. I could not walk. I could not lie down. Every step gave me a shock not unlike that which you might experience upon finding out you were adopted (or in the case of my family, upon finally coming to terms with the fact that indeed you were not). Sitting in a chair was equal to the discomfort felt by a Roman Catholic in a Southern Baptist tent revival. If I tried to lay upon my bed, I tossed and turned like Confederate bones buried in the floor of a Yankee prison. One afternoon I hobbled around town to complete a few errands. I presented such a pitiful figure standing in line at the post office the clerk mistakenly assumed I was the model for a postage stamp featuring an image of Quasimodo from the classic novel *The Hunchback of Notre Dame.*

Between the time of my diagnosis and the formation of a treatment plan for my pain and suffering, I made the mistake of mentioning my herniated disc on social media. My friends—and I use that term very loosely—recommended, insisted upon, and swore by a holistic approach.

It was suggested I try some yoga stretches. The following instructions appeared in my digital feed:

1. Squat down on the floor until you are resting on the balls of your feet.
2. Throw your head back with your eyes aimed skyward. Do not panic if you feel momentary dizziness.
3. Once you have re-established your equilibrium, touch your left elbow to your right ear. Then touch your right elbow to your left ear. Repeat as needed.

This medieval torture technique did nothing to relieve my pain, but after achieving this twisted position I suddenly had an inexplicable craving for pretzels, the soft, gooey kind covered in cinnamon and sugar that you can buy at the mall. This foray into yoga caused me to gain nine pounds. When I lamented this fact on social media, another "friend" suggested essential oils. But I had already tried frying pretzel dough in all three of the essentials—vegetable, shortening, and lard—but I still gained weight. A third "friend" said for better health plus weight loss I should consult someone at the health food store. This was the first suggestion that seemed to have real merit. I was not convinced health food would relieve back pain, but I figured it was pretty good for weight loss, because all the people I know who eat health food look like death warmed over.

The proprietor of my local "Eat Dirt So You Won't Die" suggested I try drinking barley green. The product comes in a large plastic jar with a picture of a horse on the label. Not just any horse, a beautiful specimen of the equine species with rippling muscles, bright shining eyes, and a beautiful blonde mane flowing down its neck (think Fabio on four legs). The implication being that if you eat the food of a horse you will gain the strength of one. I enthusiastically purchased a jar of this miracle cure, carefully noting the recommended dosage printed on the back. The instructions said to mix two tablespoons of barley green into six ounces of liquid. Never being the type of person to do anything by halves, I doubled the recipe. The result was a tumbler full of sludge, much like you see when washing out the underside of a lawnmower. I decided to hold my nose and drink the whole thing straight down. I can attest to the effectiveness of barley green as a weight loss product. Indeed, I fear I threw up my immortal soul. After these experiences with holistic medicine, whenever I am asked to post an online review for yoga, essential oils, or barley green, I share my favorite Biblical quotation—"Shut up!"

Since advice from my friends was not improving my situation, I sought the services of a professional by consulting a chiropractor. Upon meeting the crack practitioner, I extended my hand. He ignored my genteel gesture and instead took my chin firmly in his grip. He turned my head very slowly to the left, then to the right. I was expecting to hear the snap of my neck signaling either a cessation of my pain or blessed release in a quick death. However, that was not what happened at all.

With my chin still in his hand he began staring into my eyes. He held the gaze for a ridiculously long period of time, to the point that I became uncomfortable. Finally, I asked him what he was doing and he informed me that by studying the color pattern in the iris of my eye he could tell whether I had a swollen prostate. I quickly informed him we had just met and I was not at all comfortable with this level of intimacy. Besides, my prostate wasn't my problem; I suffered from a herniated disc and had the mammogram to prove it. Upon learning I had already been diagnosed, he suggested electro-shock therapy. I was skeptical as that particular form of treatment had already been tried on several members of my family without yielding any visible sign of improvement. I informed him of this fact, but he assured me this was different.

The chiropractor had me lie down on a padded table and put my face in a donut-shaped pillow very similar to the ones they give you to sit on after hemorrhoid surgery. (Don't ask me how I know that.) Then the chiropractor attached some electrodes to my lower back. Wow! When I left his office and walked down the street, I looked like Quasimodo starring in *Saturday Night Fever.* I'm telling you, if I ever suffer another herniated disc and my choices of treatments are electro-shock therapy or an earthquake, I'll take my chances with the earthquake.

My experience with chiropractic medicine was so traumatic I was forced to seek the help of a hypnotherapist. (If you want to see the very definition of desperate, take a look at the people sitting in the waiting room of the hypnotherapist.) When I was called back I found myself in a candlelit room with sitar music playing in the background. I sat in a beanbag opposite the therapist. We were facing each other, very close, knee to knee.

She began by asking, "On what part of your body do you wish for me to concentrate?"

I quickly stood and said, "You're not my type, but I know a chiropractor who might be interested."

The hypnotherapist remained calm and explained, "The idea is to refocus the brain, to concentrate on a part of the body that is *not* in pain, thereby creating a positive energy."

I sat back down. As I did so, I placed my hands on my knees.

She spoke in a soft, quiet tone. "Let's focus on your hands. I'm going to tell you a little story and you look only at your hands. If you begin to get sleepy, close your eyes and listen to the story as you continue to think about your hands."

It wasn't long before my eyelids grew heavy and I was dreaming about ... Suddenly a timer dinged.

"Your time is up."

I have no idea if it worked. All I know is since my visit to the hypnotherapist, whenever I hear a bell ring I shove my hand into my vest and start singing the French national anthem.

Finally, my original doctor asked me to return to his office. There was no explanation as to why it took so long for him to come up with a plan for treatment. I highly suspect it required an act of Congress to provide the necessary motivation for my insurance company, but we will never know since the Senate committee hearing took place behind closed doors. The plan turned out to be a steroid shot. A nurse checked me over, noting my blood pressure was elevated, which was to be expected since I am a bit hesitant when it comes to needles. Without further ado, I was ushered into a small room and again required to lay down on a table and place my face into a hemorrhoid donut. The doctor was holding a very small syringe, perhaps two inches long.

"Oh, this isn't going to be so bad," I commented with much relief.

He quickly set me straight. "No, this is the Valium we administer to calm you down. After it takes effect we use this." He picked up a syringe that looked like Stonewall Jackson's sword, but add six inches.

I was incredulous. "Why did you show me that?"

His answer was not at all comforting, but it did confirm my suspicions about the Senate committee hearing. "Generally we set up a screen to keep you from seeing, but your insurance isn't so good and they wouldn't pay for it." Without any more conversation he administered the Valium. Then he employed General Jackson's sword. "Can you feel that?"

Sacre bleu! I responded by singing the French national anthem ... in Swahili! I'm sorry to say the steroid shot, like most acts of Congress, was painful but ineffective. Three weeks later, I was informed by the doctor that I must "go under the knife," which is preferable to being impaled with a weapon from the Civil War, I assure you.

While I awaited the scheduled date of my execution, the doctor employed a lobbyist to railroad a piece of legislation through sub-committee with my insurance company that provided a bottle of pain medication. Y'all! Before the introduction of this elixir the world was gray and dull, but now colors were never so bright. I still hurt, but I didn't care. However, there were unavoidable side effects. The medication caused me to be overly emotional. One night I limped into the kitchen, poured myself a glass of water, and popped a couple pills. Then I eased down into my recliner. With my cell phone in hand, I put in some earbuds. When my wife asked what I was doing, I explained that in about thirty minutes, when the medication started to flow through my bloodstream, I would become emotionally distraught. So I was just going to lie back and listen to a recording of Handel's *Messiah* sung by the Mormon Tabernacle Choir and have myself a good cry.

Before I could be carried away by the glorious sounds of an Oxy oratorio, my cell phone rang. It was a representative of my insurance company calling to ask if I would be willing to delay surgery for another three or four days while he searched for a cheaper hospital. I was ready to kill him, but I couldn't murder him over the phone. So I resorted to the next best thing. "Sir, I very much want to discuss this matter, but I'm in a terrible amount of pain which makes it difficult for me to concentrate. Please do me the favor of calling back in about thirty minutes when my meds have taken full effect."

After ending the call, I popped two more of my Mormon Tabernacle pills, drank a glass of water, and returned to my recliner to await the return phone call.

When he called back, I should have recorded it, because my tearful rant was worthy of an Oscar nomination.

"Let me tell you something! I swallowed barley green and threw up my immortal soul. Then I was under the care of a chiropractor who was entirely too fresh. A hypnotherapist permanently altered my mental state. Finally, I had a needle resembling Stonewall Jackson's sword sheathed in my sciatic nerve. So no, I will not delay surgery while you look for a cheaper facility. If you have depleted the resources provided to you by my special act of Congress, then I suggest you cash in some bitcoin, try your hand at the lottery, or cozy up to the dictator of a Banana Republic, because YOU ARE GOING TO PAY FOR THIS PROCEDURE!"

When I paused to take a breath, the insurance agent meekly said, "You know what? I'm just going to stamp 'PRE-APPPROVED' on the top of your folder. In fact, I'm going to pre-approve you for any procedure you may ever need for as long as you have a relationship with this company."

"Hallelujah! And you better send me a copy of that in writing, because I'm going to hold your company to it forever and ever and ever and ever!"

As I ended the call I felt very accomplished having delivered both an Academy Award winning speech and a rendition of the Hallelujah Chorus that was worthy of a Grammy. But my wife, being a music teacher, simply shouted, "Shut up!"

On the momentous day of my surgery, I lay waiting in the prep room for the anesthesiologist to step in and deliver the customary speech peppered with phrases like "You're in good hands." "I'll be with you the whole time." "Make sure you stay with me." "Don't go toward the light."

Eventually, a gentleman dressed in surgical scrubs entered. Consulting a clipboard he looked at me and said, "Good morning. How's that knee doing today?"

I quickly informed him it was not my knee, but my back that required treatment, but he proceeded to take out a black magic marker to brand the knee cap he planned to replace. I was unprepared to deliver another dramatic oratorio. Besides, I was not allowed to have my cell phone, so there was no recording of the Mormon Tabernacle Choir to back me up. For lack of a better option, I simply screamed. This brought a nurse running. She took one look at the doctor, rolled her eyes, and handed him a pair of reading glasses.

Looking through the corrective lenses, he glanced back down at his clipboard. "Sorry, wrong room!"

(As a storyteller, I tend to color things up a bit, but this incident actually happened just as I have related it. I share this story so if you should ever require surgery you can be prepared. Leave the cell phone but take the gun.)

Finally, my doctor came into the prep room. When I told him about the aforementioned fiasco he assured me that ... The anesthesia took effect before I heard the end of his words. If you have ever had surgery, you know how one drifts off. If you haven't, go get something done, because that is the best sleep you will ever have in your life. I highly recommend it.

Waking in recovery, my vision was a little blurry. As things came into focus I recognized the nurse who had rescued me from a knee replacement. I expressed some anxiety and she assured me I had undergone treatment for a herniated disc, not an accidental hysterectomy. When an orderly came to wheel me away to a private room she cautioned, "This one is overly emotional. Don't be alarmed if he sings the French national anthem or the Hallelujah Chorus."

I spent the night in the hospital without incident.

The next morning my surgeon came into the room, proclaimed my surgery a success, and encouraged me to become ambulatory once again. He instructed me to slowly sit up on the edge of the bed, then stand holding his arm for extra support. With this task accomplished, he presented me with a sort of girdle. Wrapping it around my midsection, he stepped behind me. As I clutched a bedrail in a similar fashion to Scarlet O'Hara, he began cinching up the laces on my corset.

"Now, let's take a little walk down the hall."

Since I was trussed up like a hussy I suggested we accessorize with a pair of stiletto heels and a feather boa so I could walk the street, but the doctor didn't want me to overexert myself and said a short stroll around the hallway would suffice. After our short walk, he released me to return home with instructions to wear the back brace at all times. I asked him if I could take it off in the shower.

He said, "Yes, but keep the stiletto heels on."

Of course he was joking, but he did emphatically remind me that I could not, under any circumstances, bend over. Do you realize how many times you drop the soap in the shower when you cannot bend over? But I managed by utilizing the soap-on-a-rope my children had given me as a Father's Day gift twelve years prior.

After showering came the challenge of getting dressed. Unable to bend over, putting on my underwear required an equal amount of ingenuity. My plan was simple. I would throw my shorts onto the floor, then lightly step into them. My doctor had given me a walking cane to use for extra balance. I would turn the cane upside down and use the handle as a hook to grab my shorts and pull them up where they belonged. The execution of this delicate procedure went as planned until I got my big toe hung up in the waistband of my underwear. Suddenly the waistband snapped loose, causing the cane to shoot upward at a very rapid rate. I've always said if there was such a thing as reincarnation, I wanted to return as a soprano opera singer. Well, I had a near-death experience trying to put on my underwear with that walking stick.

At my first post-op visit I mentioned this predicament to the doctor and reminded him I was pre-approved by my insurance company for anything I wanted. Consequently, he prescribed two assistants: a home healthcare nurse to help me with my underwear plus a ghost writer to pen this tale while I recuperated from back surgery. So as it turns out, what folks predicted was one-hundred percent correct—I got a good story out of it.

WORTERMELON TIME

Poem by James Whitcomb Riley
Stories by Tim Lowry

Old wortermelon time is a-comin' round ag'in,
And they ain't no man a-livin' any tickleder'n me,
Fer the way I hanker after wortermelons is a sin -
Which is the why and wharefore, as you can plainly see.

Oh! it's in the sandy soil wortermelons does the best,
And it's thare they'll lay and waller in the sunshine and the dew
Tel they wear all the green streaks clean off of theyr breast;
And you bet I ain't a-findin' any fault with them; air you?

They ain't no better thing in the vegetable line;
And they don't need much 'tendin', as ev'ry farmer knows;
And when theyr ripe and ready fer to pluck from the vine,
I want to say to you theyr the best fruit that grows.

It's some likes the yeller-core, and some likes the red,
And it's some says "The Little Californy" is the best;
But the sweetest slice of all I ever wedged in my head,
Is the old "Edingburg Mounting-sprout," of the west.

Seems like everybody has an opinion about what kind of watermelon is best. My uncle Bill Miles certainly did. He was a cotton farmer from Mississippi, or as he pronounced it, "Miss Sippi." He was married to my mother's sister, Helen, but everybody called her Sissy.

"Uncle Bill Miles and dear Aunt Sissy, live down south with Ol' Miss Sippi!" Sorry, that's a thing we used to say. Family joke.

Anyway, like I was saying, Uncle Bill Miles had a definite opinion about watermelons. He always insisted on a Georgia Rattlesnake. I don't like them on account of the name. It just conjures up a horrible image in my mind. As a child, whenever I saw a picture of a snake in a book, I would turn the page with a fork. But Uncle Bill Miles insisted the best melon was a Georgia Rattlesnake melon.

One time when were visiting our relatives in Ol' Miss Sippi and I was about six, my Uncle Bill said to me, "Tammy!" (That's what he always called me. Not "Timmy" but "Tammy." I suppose it was a Miss Sippi thing.) "Tammy, I'm going to take you for a ride in my truck to the hardware store and buy you a toy tractor."

I remember those special trips to the hardware store. In Miss Sippi when your old folks wanted to show you off to their friends, the aunts would take their nieces to church, and the uncles would take their young nephews to the hardware store.

As we were riding along in his pickup truck Uncle Bill asked, "What kind of tractor do you want?"

Well, I was familiar with John Deere, so I said, "I want one of those green tractors with yellow wheels."

Uncle Bill Miles hit the brakes. "Uh-uh! I'm an International man. You're going to get a red tractor!"

I guess he had definite opinions about lots of things. So we went on to the hardware store and sure enough, he bought me a big, red, toy tractor. It was a beautiful International with a covered cab and a steering wheel that really turned. Uncle Bill lifted me and my new tractor into the cab of his truck and we started back to his home.

On the roadside we spotted a produce stand selling watermelons. He says to me, "Now you have to be careful how you ask about the origin of a watermelon, because they'll tell you whatever they think you want to hear."

He pulled over to the side of the road, rolled down his truck window, and hollered to the teenager working the produce stand, "I say, young man!" (Uncle Bill really did talk like that, like Foghorn Leghorn.) "I say, young man, are those Florida melons you're selling there?"

The boy answered enthusiastically, "Oh, yes sir! These are fine Florida melons straight from Tallahassee. Very fresh. They were picked out of the fields just yesterday."

Uncle Bill spit a stream of tobacco juice out the truck window and said, "Thank you, but I prefer a Georgia Rattlesnake melon myself." He rolled up the truck window and drove away.

"Why don't you want a Florida watermelon?" I asked.

"Them boys in Tallahassee plow their fields with tractors what got yellow wheels!"

You don't want no punkins nigh your wortermelon vines -
'Cause, some-way-another, they'll spile your melons, shore;
I've seed 'em taste like punkins, from the core to the rines,
Which may be a fact you have heerd of before.

But your melons that's raised right and 'tended to with care,
You can walk around amongst 'em with a parent's pride and joy,
And thump 'em on the heads with as fatherly a air
As ef each one of them was your little girl er boy.

Everybody has their own way of choosing a watermelon. My daddy was a thumper. Some people study the
stems, some people count the stripes; but my daddy, he
thumped the melon and listened for ripeness. Just once, I
wished something from the inside of a watermelon would
have thumped back!

When I was about ten years old we went on a family
vacation. With the pop-up camper hitched to the back of
the car, we were off to Corbin, Kentucky to spend several
days in the campground at Cumberland Falls State Park.
As we were driving, we saw a fruit stand on the side of the
road with watermelons for sale.

Daddy said, "Oh, let's stop and get a watermelon for
our Fourth of July picnic!"

We pulled over and he climbed out of the car. There were several melons on the ground by the side of the road, but he asked the farmer if he could climb up in the truck and select his own because he wanted to do some thumping.

The farmer said, "Knock yourself out."

My daddy climbed up and started thumping on this one and thumping on that one. And of course, my sister and I are sitting in the back of the car yelling, "Hurry up! It's hot! We wanna go!"

Finally Dad picked one that sounded just right. He jumped down from the bed of the truck, but with that big ol' melon cradled against his chest he didn't see where he was about to land. When he hit the ground he accidentally stomped right through one of the melons displayed by the roadside. That's how he ended up paying for two melons, the one he wanted and the one he squashed under his size twelve hiking boot.

He put our melon in the back of the car and started to pull back out onto the highway. He completely forgot about allowing extra clearance for the pop-up camper hitched to the back of the car. The camper clipped another melon on the ground and smashed it flat, red juice splattering out on the highway.

My dad didn't even realize it, so he kept driving, but my sister and I looked out the back window and saw the farmer throw his hat on the ground.

"Daddy, you ran over another melon."

He looked in the rearview mirror and saw the farmer standing in the road cussing and yelling. We drove to a wide spot in the road, turned around, went back, and my daddy paid for a second squashed watermelon. When we arrived at our campsite, Dad set the surviving melon on top of a picnic table, then got busy popping up the camper.

I noticed the picnic table was right on the edge of a long, steep bank that went down to a creek full of rocks. I don't really know why, but I turned to my mom and said, "I wonder what would happen if that melon rolled off the end of this picnic table and down to the creek."

My mother lifted her foot and put it against the watermelon as she said, "There's only one sure way to find out."

She gave the melon a shove. It rolled off the table, onto the ground, and down the bank to the creek bed, where it splattered to pieces on a big, flat rock.

My daddy looked up from his work with the pop-up camper. "What did you do that for?"

My mom replied matter-of-factly, "You were born in the South, you should know death comes in threes. That melon just needed killing!"

I joy in my hart jest to hear that rippin' sound
When you split one down the back and jolt the halves in two,
And the friends you love the best is gethered all around -
And you says unto your sweethart, "Oh, here's the core fer you!"

And I like to slice 'em up in big pieces fer 'em all,
Espeshally the childern, and watch theyr high delight
As one by one the rines with theyr pink notches falls,
And they holler fer some more, with unquenched appetite.

Boys takes to it natchurl, and I like to see 'em eat -
A slice of wortermelon's like a frenchharp in theyr hands,
And when they "saw" it through theyr mouth sich music can't be beat -
'Cause it's music both the sperit and the stummick understands.

My friend Trina used to go on family trips to visit her grandmother. She and her brother Nicky always looked forward to stopping at this little roadside fruit stand called the Dog Patch on their way. Their daddy always selected the watermelon too, but unlike my dad, he was a plugger, not a thumper. He would use his pocket knife to cut a little plug out of a melon and taste it. If it wasn't any good, he'd just stick the rind back into the hole, roll the melon over a bit to cover the plug, and select another one. Trina told me one time her daddy bought a watermelon at the Dog Patch and put it on the floor of the car behind the driver's seat. The next time they stopped, it was at a fast food restaurant, and her brother Nicky snatched two extra straws. When they started off on the next leg of their trip, those two kids pulled the plug out, stuck the straws into the melon, and started sucking. By the time they got to their granny's house they had sucked that melon dry, but they had put the plug back in and never let on. Later that night their grandmother wondered why they kept getting up to go to the bathroom. She figured it out a couple days later when she sliced open the melon and it was snow white on the inside!

> *Oh, they's more in wortermelons than the purty-colored meat,*
> *And the overflowin' sweetness of the worter squshed betwixt*
> *The up'ard and the down'ard motions of a feller's teeth,*
> *And it's the taste of ripe old age and juicy childhood mixed.*
>
> *Fer I never taste a melon but my thoughts flies away*
> *To the summertime of youth; and again I see the dawn,*
> *And the fadin' afternoon of the long summer day,*
> *And the dusk and dew a-fallin', and the night a-comin' on.*
>
> *And thare's the corn around us, and the lispin' leaves and trees,*
> *And the stars a-peekin' down on us as still as silver mice,*
> *And us boys in the wortermelons on our hands and knees,*
> *And the new-moon hangin' ore us like a yeller-cored slice.*
>
> *Oh! it's wortermelon time is a-comin' round again,*
> *And they ain't no man a-livin' any tickleder'n me,*
> *Fer the way I hanker after wortermelons is a sin -*
> *Which is the why and wharefore, as you can plainly see.*

Folks often say to me, "I don't have any good family stories like you." But I don't believe that, not for one minute. Everybody's got good family stories. Start with watermelon. If that doesn't get the conversation going, pull out a Georgia rattlesnake.

249

OLD FOLKS AT THE DMV

It was time to renew my driver's license, which required a visit to the Department of Motor Vehicles. I took my number and sat down to begin the aging process. Looking over the crowded waiting room I could see everyone else had resigned themselves to the same fate. People were reading paperback novels or scrolling on their smartphones, passing the time, waiting for their service number to be called, or perchance to grow old and die. The odds were about the same.

I looked back toward the entrance to see an old gentleman come walking through the door. It was August, at least a hundred degrees in the shade, and he's wearing a dark, flannel suit, a tie, and a fedora. He shuffles up to the reception desk and announces in a loud voice, "I'm eighty-five years old!"

I thought to myself, *What a good idea! Announce your advanced age right off and maybe they will realize the chances of you surviving the wait time are slim to none and they will bump you to the head of the line.*

The receptionist said, "Excuse me?"

The gentleman repeated, "I'm eighty-five years old!"

"Yes, sir. How can I help you?"

"I'm here to renew my driver's license. My wife is with me. She's parking the car."

The receptionist nodded. "Here's your number." She handed him a ticket and he shuffled over to a row of plastic chairs but did not sit down. He stood there for a full minute. Finally, the receptionist said, "Sir, you can sit down."

"My wife. She's parking the car."

After another minute a thin lady with white hair entered the waiting area. She was wearing a flowery dress made from chintz fabric reminiscent of old-fashioned blue-plate china. A patent leather purse hung from the crook of her arm and she wore a hat. The husband and wife sat down together.

Finally, an automated voice announced in a soulless drone, "Now serving number four seventy-two."

Something was mixed up. They had called his number before they called mine. But I didn't complain, I just thought *Well, it worked. Next time I have to come here, I'm going to tell them I'm eighty-five years old.*

The gentleman stood and walked to the tall service counter. A young woman stood on the other side, looking down at him. He announced, "I'm eighty-five years old!" as he lay his expired license on the counter.

"Yes, sir," she replied.

Then she explained to the gentleman that a vision test was required of all senior citizens renewing a driver's license. He answered, "Yes. Yes, I am prepared."

The woman got the viewfinder ready and instructed, "Now, just look into this little window right here and tell me what you see." The gentleman put his face up to the viewfinder but didn't say anything. The woman asked, "What do you see?"

"I see an E."

"Yes, that's the largest letter. It's just a single E on the first line. Can you read the next line?"

He checked again. "I can't see that."

The young woman picked up the gentleman's expired driver's license. She studied it for just a second, then said, "It says here you're required to wear corrective lenses. You don't have contact lenses, do you?"

He said, "No. No, I wear glasses."

"Well, you should wear your glasses when you take this vision test."

He looked pleased and said, "Oh, am I allowed to wear my glasses?"

"Yes, sir!" And then she thoughtfully added, "And you should always wear them whenever you are driving your car."

The gentleman walked back over to his wife and said, "I need my eyeballs."

The white-haired lady popped open her patent leather purse, took out a glasses case, slid out a pair of glasses, carefully shined each lens with a lace-bordered handkerchief, then handed the spectacles to her husband. He put them on. He walked back. He put his eyes up to the viewfinder.

"I see an E."

The employee asked, "You can't see the next line?"

"No, I can't see the next line."

The young woman frowned, then she brightened. "Is your prescription up to date? Are these your newest pair of glasses?"

He replied with just the slightest ray of hope, "I have reading glasses."

"Well, let's try those."

The gentleman walked back over to his wife. "I need my other eyeballs."

She took out a second pair of glasses, shined each lens with her lace-bordered handkerchief, and handed them to her husband. He put them on top the first pair still on his face. When he looked up, his huge eyeballs were swimming in two magnified pools. He walked back, looked through the viewfinder.

"I see two Es."

The young woman took a deep breath, then spoke loudly and clearly. Everybody could hear. "I'm very sorry to inform you, but I cannot renew your driver's license." She picked up a giant pair of scissors and cut his license in half.

The gentleman stared at the two pieces of plastic that lay on the counter. He took off one pair of glasses, and then the other. Standing with a pair in each hand he looked straight at the young woman and said, "Thank you." Then he walked back to his wife and handed her the glasses. He stood watching as his wife slid them into their respective cases, placed the cases into her patent leather purse, and snapped it shut. With finality, he said, "We can go now."

The white-haired lady stood and took her husband's arm. The waiting room was silent. They walked its entire length, together.

Approaching the exit he announced, "I can't hear. I can't see. And now I can't drive. I don't know how you're going to get to the Piggly Wiggly."

The lady opened the door for her husband. After he stepped through, she turned back slightly, her voice directed toward those of us left to wait in the Department of Motor Vehicles.

"That's all right. You're still my Robert, and I love you."

TELLING STORIES

MY PAL PAM

Just before I graduated high school, my drama teacher sat me down for a serious conversation. "You know, I always do my best to talk students out of majoring in theater when they go off to college. It's a hard way to make a living. I usually recommend kids pursue it as a hobby and major in something else, anything that will lead to stable employment and a steady income. I'm not going to give you my regular advice, but I will continue to keep an eye on you."

All the other students called our drama teacher "Miss Holcomb," but to me she was just "Pam," and she had been keeping an eye on me for just about as long as I could remember.

I am often asked how one learns to be a good storyteller. I always answer that question by saying, "Storytellers are not taught, they are grown." Theater is life. Storytelling is the human experience. However, nobody gives workshops or PowerPoint presentations on how to be a human. The best I can do is tell you how my pal Pam helped me grow up to become a storyteller.

You can count the key points of being a storyteller on the fingers of one hand. A good storyteller must be creative, committed, courageous, and keen-eyed. Finally, and most importantly, a good storyteller—any good human actually—must remember a person should never go too far. Let me explain.

A GOOD STORYTELLER MUST BE CREATIVE.

Right after I turned five, my daddy was hired as the new pastor of Putney Bible Baptist Church in Harlan, Kentucky. It took my family a couple weeks to move into the parsonage, pull all our stuff out of the packing boxes, and arrange everything just the way we wanted. One of the last things to be unpacked was my mom's collection of salt and pepper shakers. I'm sure my mother had been collecting them from the time before us kids were even born. She had salt and pepper shakers of every shape, size, and color. My three-year-old sister and I sat on the couch and watched my mom carefully unwind the bubble wrap from thirty or forty sets, then carefully place each pair on the shelves in a display cabinet with sliding glass doors my dad had mounted on the living room wall. There were all sorts of animal pairs: a black dog for pepper and a white cat for salt, a porcelain hen with a matching rooster, a pair of country pigs in overalls. There were porcelain people too. I remember a couple of Mexican fellows wearing serapes and sombreros. Charlie Brown and his dog Snoopy were my particular favorites. And I also remember two little green frogs. When my mother slid the glass doors closed, she reminded us we were never to touch the salt and pepper shakers. We took her admonition very seriously, but we couldn't have touched them even if we wanted to because Dad had hung the cabinet high on the wall, well out of our reach.

After the house was in order, my parents wanted to go out one evening for dinner. They hired a high school senior whose family attended our church to babysit my sister and me. When the babysitter came to the house, she told us her name was Pam. After my parents left, Pam played with us for a little while. Then she heated up the frozen TV dinners my mom had set out for our supper. Finally, she helped us take baths and get into our pajamas. She told us if we hurried, there would be enough time for a story before we went to bed. Being little kids, we didn't realize Pam was a drama student at the local high school. She had been practicing a Brer Rabbit story for a speech competition and wanted to try out her piece on us. My sister and I were sitting with Pam on the couch, ready for our story, when she looked at the salt and pepper shaker cabinet on the wall across the room.

"Oh look, one of your momma's little green frogs has gotten turned around backward."

Even though we had only lived in this new house for a couple weeks, we had already become accustomed to things getting jostled around from time to time on account of some road construction taking place across the valley from our home. Engineers were cutting a new highway through the mountain. Every time they set off dynamite to blast away the rock, the house would shake, windows would rattle, and small things, like salt and pepper shakers, would wobble. Pam stood up from the couch, walked over to the display cabinet, slid the glass doors open, and reached in to turn the little green frog around so it would be facing forward. Unfortunately, the blasting had not only wobbled the little green frog, it had also loosened the hook anchoring the cabinet to the wall, and the whole thing fell off into Pam's arms, with salt and pepper shakers crashing to the floor and shattering into hundreds of little pieces.

Pam sucked in a quick breath, then turned toward us kids sitting on the couch in our pajamas and bare feet. "Don't move!" She carefully tip-toed through the bits of porcelain to set the cabinet and its remaining contents on the floor. Then she went into the kitchen and grabbed the phone to call her girlfriend, Gina. (Time does not afford me the opportunity to tell you all about Gina Johnson. Suffice to say Pam and Gina could have given Laverne and Shirley a run for their money.)

We heard Pam say, "Gina, do you have any glue? Bring every bottle you've got and get to the preacher's house as fast as you can!" After she hung up the phone, she started carefully collecting the pieces and setting them on the coffee table. My sister and I still sat on the couch, not moving a muscle. I don't know how long it took, but it seemed like mere minutes before Gina arrived with two great big bottles of Elmer's glue. In no time at all, those two teen-agers were sitting on the floor at either end of the coffee table, which Pam had covered in newspaper, painstakingly gluing all those little figurines back together.

After things had settled down a bit and Pam and Gina were busy concentrating on their task, my sister spoke from her place on the couch. "Oh, Pam! My mommy said never touch those salt and pepper shakers. Never touch them. And my daddy is going to be so mad."

Pam didn't look up. She just kept working to get a little Mexican man's head glued back onto his shoulders. Gina was trying to reattach the wing on a porcelain chicken.

My sister kept talking. "My daddy is a preacher, but when he gets mad, he says things a preacher is not sup-posed to say. He is going to say a lot."

Pam stopped long enough to look up at Gina. Gina looked back at her and saw her eyes well with tears. She tried to comfort her friend by saying, "At least you saved the little green frog."

My sister turned on Gina. "My daddy will not think that's funny. He is not funny. I do not have a funny daddy when you touch stuff." Pam's hands began to tremble. I felt sorry for her, but my sister just kept talking. "When my mommy says don't touch stuff, my daddy gets really mad when you touch stuff."

Pam got up from the floor and walked into the kitch-en. She came back with a large spoon. Sitting back down to her work, she picked up one of the bottles, squirted the spoon full of glue, then set the spoon on the table in front of my sister. Before she resumed piecing figurines back together, she said, "Have you ever eaten glue? I reckon every little kid has wanted to eat glue." Then she turned back to her task, and my sister didn't say another word. I didn't say a word either. Not because I was afraid Pam would make me eat glue, but because I was in awe. Anyone who could so creatively shut my sister up would be my friend for life!

A good storyteller must be creative. But I didn't learn that in drama class. Pam taught me that with a spoon and a big bottle of Elmer's glue.

Just in case you're wondering, Gina stayed with Pam until my mom and dad came home. She stood by her friend's side as Pam tearfully told my parents what had happened. I noticed neither of them mentioned the spoon full of glue. When the story was concluded, my mom just reached out to give Pam a hug and she thanked Gina for being such a loyal friend.

Then she said, "I'm sorry you girls went to so much trouble. These are just worthless knick-knacks I mostly bought at yard sales."

Without another word, she bent down, scooped up the newspaper and all the salt and pepper shakers Pam and Gina had so painstakingly glued back together, rolled the whole mess into a ball, and threw it into the trash. Pam breathed a big sigh of relief while my sister sat there on the couch with her mouth gaping open.

I couldn't wait for Pam to babysit us again! And she did, lots of times, but eventually she graduated from high school and went off to study theater as a college student at Lincoln Memorial University in Harrogate, Tennessee.

One year at Christmastime, when Pam was home from school and I was about eight, my dad tapped her to direct the annual Sunday School pageant. Well, this was not going to be the typical bathrobe drama with a few recitations and a bunch of little angels singing "Silent Night" to a plastic baby doll. No sir! We had a real director who was committed to the theatrical arts and chose a two-act play with an intermission and everything! Pam asked me to commit to the role of a shepherd boy named Benjamin.

A GOOD STORYTELLER MUST BE COMMITTED.

I had never been in a play before, but after just a few rehearsals I quickly decided acting a part was very easy. I memorized my lines without any trouble, and at play practice, I would march onto the stage, plant my feet, and rattle off my speech in a robotic voice: "Hark, a star appears in the eastern sky. It seems to shine over Bethlehem. Let us leave these sheep to graze upon the hillside while we go and see this wonderous site." With each rehearsal my speech got faster and faster and faster. Soon, you couldn't understand a word I was saying. And it's not bragging to say I was the best actor in the cast.

Poor Pam was growing increasingly frustrated as she tried to wring a dramatic performance out of a Sunday School class full of ragtag mannequins delivering pre-recorded messages about the birth of Jesus. At the conclusion of the final dress rehearsal, she sat us all down and tried to articulate her directorial vision. "You're not just quoting lines to see who can say things the fastest. You must commit to the character. Before you speak the words of a shepherd, you must *be* a shepherd. You must walk like a shepherd, you must talk like a shepherd, breathe like a shepherd, think like a shepherd. Do you understand?"

We did not.

She tried to illustrate with an example from her own experience. "Last semester at school my acting partner and I had to commit to playing sea monsters. We wore green body suits and painted green makeup all over our faces, but it wasn't enough to just look like monsters. We had to act like monsters, all the time, even when we were not speaking. We had to sit around on a big rock and flick our tongues in and out like two lizard people. We had to be fully committed to being sea monsters. I need you to be fully committed to being a shepherd or a wiseman or Mary or Joseph or whoever you are playing. All the time. Whether you are talking or not."

I really took Pam's coaching to heart. The next night I walked out into the light, pointed toward the cardboard star hanging from the ceiling above the stage, and began to quote my lines with the best sea monster commitment I could muster. "Hark, a star appears in the eastern sky. (tongue flick, tongue flick) It seems to shine over Bethlehem. (tongue flick) Let us leave these sheep (tongue flick) to graze upon the hillside (tongue flick) while we go (tongue flick) and see this wonderous site." (tongue flick, tongue flick, tongue flick)

Of course, the audience was more than a little amused. Pam got a good laugh out of it too, but my dad could never talk her into directing another church Christmas play. Eventually I learned what it meant to be committed to the character you were playing and the story you wanted to tell, but I first discovered it in my pal Pam's original Christmas drama featuring shepherds, wisemen, the Holy Family, and The Creature from The Black Lagoon.

By the time I was in middle school, Pam had graduated college and was teaching drama at the local high school. She would let me tag along to play rehearsals and speech tournaments, and I learned plenty by observing her more advanced students. I also learned a lot just by hanging around with her as a friend. I often spent Saturday afternoons with Pam doing whatever—mowing the grass, playing board games, watching movies, or just talking.

One day when we were hanging out, Pam asked, "Did you hear about Chris's grandma?" Chris was a good friend; we went to school and church together, and I knew his grandma had recently died. "Are you going to the funeral?"

"No," I answered, very committedly I might add.

She pressed for a reason. "Why?"

"Because I've never been to a funeral, and I don't want to see a dead person."

Pam was shocked the preacher's kid had never attended a funeral, but I assured her I had not and I did not plan to go to this one. "Well that's just dumb," she pronounced. "You should go and support your buddy, Chris. Besides, someday your grandma will die, and you don't want that to be the very first time you ever set foot in a funeral home, do you? If you're uncomfortable, I'll go with you." Pam was helping me to be courageous.

A GOOD STORYTELLER MUST BE COURAGEOUS.

Surveys often show that people fear public speaking more than death itself. For me, it was the other way around, but Pam helped me get over it.

I was still insisting I wasn't going to the funeral when she said, "If I can go whitewater rafting with you, then you can go to the funeral home with me."

Well, she had me there. One summer Pam had volunteered to chaperone a field trip when our church youth group went whitewater rafting in the New River Gorge in West Virginia. When we got to a particular point on our trip down the river, our guide told us the next cascade was known as a swimmer's rapid because it was safe to jump out of the boat and ride the waves like a body surfer at the beach. As our boat approached the white, choppy water, he reminded us that with our life jackets on we would readily float, no danger whatsoever. Reassured, all of us teenagers jumped over the side of the big rubber raft, and Pam followed. Sure enough, we bobbed along like rubber ducks floating in a giant sloshing bathtub.

Except for Pam. I don't understand it. She was wearing a life jacket, but somehow managed to go under instead of over every single wave and swallowed half the river in the process. Every time she surfaced, she would let out a scream of sheer panic, only to be nearly drowned by the next foaming swell of water. The river guide leapt from the raft and employed all his rescue skills to pull her out of the current. By the time we hauled her back into the boat, she was hyperventilating.

After several minutes, when she finally caught her breath, the river guide said, "We got you. You're ok. Just concentrate on your breathing and getting your heart rate down."

Pam looked up at everyone gathered around and informed us, "I don't know how to swim." We immediately wanted to know why she had jumped into the river. "Well, I figured it was safe with a life jacket, so I thought this would be a good time to face my fear."

After that incident, Pam could make me do anything by saying, "If I can go whitewater rafting, you can ..." Fill in the blank.

I dropped my argument and that evening we went to the funeral home, just for the viewing. Pam said that would be good enough. When we walked in, I immediately saw my friend Chris. He looked up and said, "Hey." I returned a "hey." And that was pretty much it, because that's all middle school boys ever say to each other in most any circumstance, including the viewing for a deceased grandmother. Pam shook hands with Chris and offered her condolences.

That wasn't bad, but then she turned to me and said, "Now we're going into the next room to view the body."

And I whispered, "I wish I had a life jacket."

"Just go with the flow and I'll keep you from drowning. All you have to do is stop for a second, glance down, then move on. If you get nervous, just look at me."

I watched Pam approach the coffin, pause to gaze down at the lifeless lady in a pink dress, and step away. She motioned for me to do the same. I stepped forward. I glanced down. I was looking at a corpse and feared I was about to hyperventilate. I looked up at Pam to find her standing at the foot of the coffin looking straight at me and doing the sea monster thing—tongue flick, tongue flick, tongue flick. Instead of losing my ability to breathe, I nearly lost the ability to remain sober.

She took me by the hand and said, "Now, we go get ice cream."

Pam taught me to be courageous. In fact, whenever I perform in front of a large crowd I don't calm my nerves by imagining the audience in their underwear, I just see a bunch of dead people.

A GOOD STORYTELLER MUST BE KEEN-EYED.

Finally, after knowing Pam for nearly ten years, I entered high school and officially became her drama student. Because we knew each other so well, she was already aware of my ability to mimic people. In fact, she encouraged me to do impressions of my teachers. Learning to be a keen-eyed observer of character, I studied my teachers' mannerisms and speech patterns all the time. The chorus teacher at our school was a very artsy-fartsy fellow named Steely Veach. He always spoke with an affectation, holding his mouth sideways so all his words came out in a slow drawl.

One day in drama class I pretended to be Mr. Veach in a skit. A fellow student said, "You shouldn't make fun of him. He suffered a stroke a few years ago and that's why he talks like that."

But I knew better because I had watched him closely. Mr. Veach would eat his lunch in the cafeteria and chat with his fellow arts faculty members, talking out of one side of his mouth. But when he used his napkin to wipe his lips, he would talk out of the other side. And he always laughed through his nose. I could do a spot-on Mr. Veach.

I could also do a spot-on impression of our principal, Mr. Hensley. His thing was the intercom. He was always using the microphone. It seemed like whatever crossed his mind had to be immediately announced to the whole school. Classes were constantly being interrupted with yet another speech filled with words of wisdom from our dear leader.

One afternoon, he came on the speaker while I was in Pam's classroom. From the second he started talking, it was obvious to all of us kids what was going on. One of the custodians was running a vacuum cleaner in the school office. Consequently, Mr. Hensley could not hear himself speak. However, his mouth was right on the microphone and we could hear him just fine. He was screaming his customary introduction, "STUDENTS! PLEASE EXCUSE THIS INTERRUPTION, BUT I HAVE A VERY IMPORTANT ANNOUNCEMENT!" Pam got up from her desk and walked to the classroom door. When she opened it, we could hear hysterical laughter coming from every other classroom in the hall. I instantly knew I had a new impression to add to my repertoire.

About a week later, the intercom clicked on again when I was sitting in drama class. Mr. Hensley's voice said, "Miss Holcomb, please send Tim Lowry to the office."

I looked at Pam, who just shrugged. "Sounds serious. You better hurry down there."

I had no idea why I was being called down to the principal's office. I was always yucking it up in drama class, but I never caused a moment's trouble anywhere else, mainly because my parents would've killed me. When I walked into the school office, Mr. Hensley was leaning against the front of the desk where the intercom microphone sat in a little holder. Standing in a semi-circle behind the desk was the entire high school secretarial pool, smirking.

Mr. Hensley said, "Miss Holcomb tells me you do impressions."

"Yes, sir."

"She says you do me?"

"Yes, sir."

"So do it."

I didn't speak. I didn't move. Then one of the secretaries nodded her head. So, I grabbed the microphone, pretended to press the button and yelled in my best Josh Hensley voice, "STUDENTS! PLEASE EXCUSE THIS INTERRUPTION, BUT I HAVE A VERY IMPORTANT ANNOUNCEMENT!"

The principal said, "I do not talk like that!"

But all the secretaries burst out laughing. "Oh, yes you do!"

Then Mr. Hensley chuckled and let me in on their game. "Pam told me you did impressions and I sort of used this as a little audition. Would you attend the faculty Christmas party and do impressions of the teachers? Everybody will love it and I'll pay you twenty-five bucks."

Pam got me my first paying gig!

I learned a lot from Pam: how to be creative, committed, courageous, and keenly observant. But the most important lesson of all took place the summer before I went off to college to become a theater major, just like her. It was at the Harlan County Coal Show where I learned a person should never go too far.

A GOOD STORYTELLER SHOULD NEVER GO TOO FAR.

The Coal Show was a lot like the county fair, only much bigger. It started as a trade show for the coal mining industry with displays featuring industrial machinery, safety equipment, dump trucks, end loaders, and pretty much everything else needed to run a coal mining operation. Families started attending the trade show to see what their daddy did for a living and very quickly The Harlan County Coal Show became a three-day regional event. One of the most popular activities was to take a tour of the mock mine at the local vocational school where young men learned machine repair, safety procedures, and day-to-day operations for one of the most dangerous jobs in America. "We dig coal" was a slogan said with pride back in those days.

Pam called me up Saturday morning of the big weekend and said, "Be ready in twenty minutes. I'm coming to pick you up and we'll go together to the Coal Show."

We had a good time looking at the exhibits and eating fair food. After we had walked all over the festival grounds, we ran into Pam's brother-in-law, Britt, who taught safety and rescue at the vocational school. He told us he was getting ready to start a tour of the mock mine.

We immediately asked in unison, "Can we go?"

Britt looked at both of us with a very serious expression. "If I let you two dingbats go on this tour, you have to promise you won't goof around. I've got several officials from the Kentucky Department of Health and Safety going along, and you can't be acting stupid." Pam looked at me and shot out her tongue sea-monster style. Britt caught her and said, "I mean it."

We held up our right hands and swore we would be on our best behavior. Neither of us said so, but we were both under the assumption that since it was only a mock mine, our promise was not binding. Britt said we could ride in the man-trip as he gestured toward a long, low vehicle with multiple seats used for carrying workers down into the mine shaft. The tours of the mock mine were sponsored by the Caterpillar Corporation, so of course, the vehicle was painted bright yellow. All the seats on this strange-looking car were already taken by men in suits and hard hats. When we told Britt we couldn't find a place to sit, he ordered us to "lay in the scoop."

On the front of this machine was a giant, flat shovel used for moving coal or stone or timbers or whatever else needed to be lifted out the way. That's where we were going to ride, stretched out side by side, like two people sunning themselves at the beach. If that situation wasn't comical enough, the tour did not start at the entrance to the mock mine. No, it started about two miles per hour on the opposite side of the show grounds parking lot. Every time Britt ran over a speed bump, Pam and I would bounce like unsecured cargo in the floor of a delivery truck. People were staring as we did our best to stifle laughter. Then Pam jabbed me in the ribs with her elbow and started taunting, "Do it. Do it. Do Leach!"

Robin Leach, host of *Lifestyles of the Rich and Famous*, was the only nationally known personality for which I could do an impression. I turned to face all the people staring at us and launched into an impromptu routine. "This is *Lifestyles of the Rich and Famous*. I'm your host Robin Leach."

Pam started to snicker.

I ramped up the cheesy British accent. "You may be under the false impression that this vehicle is merely an example of common coal mining machinery. In truth, it is manufactured by an exclusive company, known to the posh jet set as 'Cat-er-pill-AR.' And what you assume to be yellow paint is actually solid gold."

Pam rolled over on one hip and started gliding her fingers across the surface of the giant shovel pretending to be a game show model. We were having a hilarious ride, and the best part was Britt was stuck in the driver's seat and couldn't get to us!

Finally, we came to the entrance to the mock mine. Leaving the brightly sunlit parking lot, we were immediately plunged into darkness. Having lost our audience,

Pam and I quieted down and waited for the tour to begin. The whole thing was set up to be very dramatic. The man-trip stopped rolling forward and a baritone voice began to play over speakers located somewhere in the blackness. "Deep beneath the majestic Kentucky mountains, brave men and women risk their lives daily to extract industrial fuel from the bowels of the earth."

As the voice began speaking, Britt turned on the headlights located on the front of the man-trip to illuminate a coal mine rescue operation depicted by mannequins arranged in a dramatic diorama. The only problem was Pam and I were laying in the scoop and the bright lights created giant silhouettes showing every contour of our bodies on the opposite wall of the mock mine. I have always been rather flat chested, but Pam was not. When the voice said, "Deep beneath the majestic Kentucky mountains," well, let's just say that was the only coal mine rescue operation that ended with suits in hard hats from the Kentucky Department of Health and Safety convulsing in a laugh riot. The baritone voice continued to narrate a story about rescue and recovery, but it was too late. Everybody on that tour was far gone, except Britt. Even through the darkness, Pam and I could feel his red, hot stare.

When the tour was over and we emerged from the mock mine, she looked over at me and said, "Run, Robin Leach! Run!"

I jumped out of that scoop and took off like Moody's goose across the parking lot. A half-hour later I met Pam at her car. "I knew Britt wouldn't kill me, because he's married to my sister and we're family; but I was genuinely concerned for your safety."

A couple weeks later, I escaped Britt's wrath by going off to college in South Carolina, and I don't think Pam visited her sister until at least Thanksgiving.

Throughout my entire college career, my high school drama teacher would come see whatever show I was involved with—Shakespeare, romantic opera, murder mystery. She was always in the front row. Usually, after the show, Pam and I would go to an all-night diner to sit up until the wee hours of the morning reminiscing about our adventures together. After I graduated, she continued to follow my career, always true to her promise to keep an eye on me.

I am not the only student of Pam Holcomb who could tell you of such adventures. She was babysitter, drama coach, teacher, mentor, and friend to thousands of kids over a twenty-seven-year career. Not long after she retired, I was invited to perform at the National Storytelling Festival. By that point I had been performing at schools and smaller events for more than a decade, but this was my big break. Even though I had rehearsed and rehearsed, all the while keeping in mind a good storyteller is creative, committed, courageous, keen-eyed, and always mindful that he should never go too far, I was more than a little nervous. But when I stepped up to the microphone and looked down to the front row, there was my pal Pam looking up at me, flicking her tongue in and out like The Creature from the Black Lagoon. And the rest—as they say—is history.

279

WAFFLE HOUSE SKETCHES

When I am on the road, I often catch meals early in the morning before a long drive or late at night after an evening performance. Waffle House is always open. I like to sit by myself and just observe the stories happening all around. Here are two of my favorites.

Atlanta, GA, 7:12 a.m.

A gray-haired gentleman opens the door for a gray-haired lady. He is wearing a hat. Several men seated on stools at the counter are wearing fishing caps, but this gentleman is dressed for town. The fishing caps turn to greet the gentleman, but they seem a little disappointed to see he is not alone. Instead of calling out his name, they just nod, sort of like awkward teenage boys who forgo fraternity foolishness when a lady is present.

The lady, dressed in a floral print and heeled shoes that are stylish but sensible asks, "Where do you usually sit?"

The gentleman glances at an empty counter stool in the line of fishing caps but steers the lady toward a booth.

A waitress lays down napkins and silverware, looks at the older lady, and teases, "Oh, goodness. Are you coming with him in the mornings now? I can't flirt with your man anymore."

The lady smiles back as she says, "Now that I'm retired, I can join my husband for breakfast every day."

The waitress, completely ignoring the gentleman, hands the lady a menu. "Oh, really? You retired? Well, congratulations! Where did you work, honey?"

The lady converses with the waitress while her husband takes the menu and pretends to be deciding on what he will order. "I was a fashion buyer for Belk department store for thirty-seven years."

"You bought clothes for Belk's? Maybe you could help me get some fashions. I tried to go to that Kohl's store the other day. Well, first thing ..." She takes a pencil from behind her ear. "You can't be bigger around than this-here pencil to find anything that'll fit you these days. I finally did find something hanging on the rack that was a purty color, but when I held that blouse up in the light, you could see slap through it! I took that thang to the checkout girl and I said, 'What is this?' She says, 'Oh, it's see-through, but we have these bras to match.' I said, 'Bras? I work at the Waffle House, not the Silver Slipper!' What do you want to eat, honey?"

The lady smiles and says she is undecided. Perhaps her husband should order first. The waitress snatches the menu out of his hand and gives it back to the lady. "Oh, I already know what he wants. Same thing every morning. He's more predictable than a see-through blouse."

The waitress cackles at her own joke, but the lady stops smiling, and the gentleman is glancing back at the fellows sitting on the counter stools. He has removed his hat and they have removed their caps as if a funeral procession is passing by. The waitress may know what he always orders, but things are never going to be the same.

✲ ✲ ✲

Asheville, NC, 11:56 p.m.

Except for a young trainee following him around like his shadow in a yellow uniform and a paper hat, Joe is working the midnight shift all by himself. Realizing it's going to be some time before Joe and his shadow get to me, I take one of the two remaining available stools at the counter and survey the diner.

Four workmen sit in the booth to my right. Based on their blue uniforms with oval name tags printed on the shirts, it's safe to assume they have come from a second-shift factory job for a late supper. It is also safe to assume each one of them grew up with what is known as "snatch and grab" brothers, because they all hug plates piled high with eggs, bacon, toast, and hash browns, holding their forks and knives like weapons wielded in a territorial dispute. Joe diplomatically reaches a coffee pot into the group and tops off each cup without challenging anyone's sovereignty or upsetting the delicate balance of power.

Two ladies in fur coats and brightly painted fingernails occupy the booth to my left. Cups of coffee share the table with a laptop computer, a tablet with scribbled notes, and a program from the local theater. Hands fly with red fingernails flashing, adding dramatic flair to exclamations of "Innovative!" and "Broadway quality!" Joe brings two plates with waffles and a bottle of syrup to fuel these journalists from the Junior League who are writing a review for the morning paper.

Two girls sit facing one another across the table in the far corner of the restaurant. The girl on the left is visibly upset, mascara streaming down her cheeks. The girl on the right is shaking a finger as she preaches, "Do you love him? That is the question before you, because he ain't never gonna change. Do you love him?"

Joe steps over to the table and hands the crying girl a stack of napkins. She begins to dab her eyes as he discreetly takes a quarter from his pocket, slips it into the jukebox, and makes a quick selection. The voice of Tammy Wynette wails out "Stand By Your Man," mercifully covering the rest of the conversation and providing some much needed privacy for the poor girl who is now reapplying her mascara. Joe returns to the grill and sends his shadow off to refill coffees around the diner.

The door opens and a cowboy of sorts steps into the busy scene. Instead of denim jeans, he is sporting polyester pants the same color as his silver-gray hair and a purple western-style shirt trimmed with faux pearl snaps.

His outfit looks brand new, but the well-worn boots inform any careful observer that this ain't his first rodeo. He walks over to the counter to take the last available seat in the diner, which happens to be the stool next to mine.

Joe looks over his shoulder from the grill and hollers, "Did you go tonight?"

"Yep."

"You gonna go again tomorrow night?"

"I reckon."

"Dancing usually works up an appetite. Looks like you could stand to eat something."

"I probably might could."

"What do you want?"

"Something from the pie cabinet."

Joe raps his metal spatula on the grill like a judge bringing his gavel down as he pronounces a sentence. "Now you know good and well a diabetic can't have chocolate pie."

"What's that little girl cutting up over there?" asks the cowboy, indicating Joe's shadow who has finished making her rounds with the coffee pot and is now standing at the end of the counter slicing tomatoes.

"She's making a salad," Joe replies.

"Can a diabetic have a salad?"

"You can have a salad."

"I want a half salad."

"You can have a whole salad if you want."

"I ain't that hungry. I only want a half salad. What kind of dressing you got?"

Joe's shadow leaves her salad-making station and comes over to talk to the cowboy. "That'll be one half salad with tomatoes. For dressing I got frainch, rainch, and seizure."

"You ain't got none of that thousand dollar dressing?"

"No, all's we got is them three I said."

"Well, I'll have a half salad with frainch and a cup of coffee."

Joe takes over the order as his shadow finishes making the salad. "You ain't gonna put sugar in the coffee are you?"

The cowboy says dejectedly, "No, I'll put a pack of the pink stuff in it."

The shadow returns with the salad and the coffee. Trying to make up for the fact that he's not allowed to have sugar, she tries to be sweet and takes time to flirt just a little. "Did you dance with a purty girl?"

"I danced with a blonde. She was an old blonde, but she was a blonde."

"I like your outfit. I bet you're a good dancer. You should be on that TV show *Dancing With The Stars*. I bet you could dance circles around them."

"No, we dance in a square. That's why they call it square dancing."

The cowboy lifts his coffee cup to his lip indicating that he doesn't wish to talk anymore. The girl leaves him to eat his food. Joe needs her to deliver several orders. The cowboy finishes his salad and stands up to go.

Joe calls out from the grill. "I'll see you."

"Not if I see you first," the cowboy counters as he walks out the door.

Joe calls his shadow over and hands her the money the cowboy left on the counter. "Now listen," he says to her in a confidential tone, "his wife died about six months ago. We were afraid of losing him too, but he's just started going back to the square dances without her. We're encouraging him as best we can. Ever since his wife died there ain't nobody to check his sugar. So when he comes in here, do not let him have chocolate pie."

The waitress puts the money into the register drawer and finally gets around to taking my order. "What can I get you?"

I answer honestly, "A friend like Joe."

HELEN KELLER ON ZOOM

On Friday, March 13, 2020, at approximately two thirty, I had just finished a day's worth of programming at a local elementary school. As I signed out in the office, the school nurse said to me, "If I were you, I would go directly from here to the grocery store to purchase two weeks' worth of food and as much toilet paper as you can get your hands on. Then go straight home. We'll see you on the other side of this pandemic."

I followed her advice, thinking I was merely going to be isolated with my family for a short time to "flatten the curve." Ten days later, I realized it was my career that had been flattened as I stood looking at a wall calendar filled with storytelling gigs all marked "CANCELLED." With tears streaming down my cheeks, I turned to face my family, saying, "I cannot tell stories on Zoom."

✻✻✻

In the spring of 2018, my family traveled with me to the Shoals Storytelling Festival in Florence, Alabama. As luck would have it, on Saturday of the festival weekend, I had nothing to do. Other storytellers were presenting sessions, but I was free until the evening concert. This afforded me the whole day with my wife and kids to explore the area.

Right after breakfast we drove up the street from our hotel to the City of Florence Visitor Center. While my wife and our two young daughters browsed the brochure racks, I went to the information desk to inquire about fun and educational family activities. Since there was no one else in line, I had my pick of three staff members. First, there was a college-age young woman sporting a ponytail and her alma mater's cheerleading outfit. True to her uniform, she was literally bouncing with excitement as she informed me she was volunteering to earn community service hours. Standing a little way from the cheerleader was a middle-aged gentleman wearing dark sunglasses and a t-shirt that read "Don't drink and drive. You might hit a bump and spill your drink." I got the distinct impression he had not readily volunteered, but nonetheless was also there to fulfill a community service obligation. Finally, sitting on a tall stool at the far end of the counter was a lady dressed all in purple—blouse, pants, shoes, earrings, fingernails, the works.

I chose to speak to the cheerleader because she seemed the most eager to be helpful and I appreciated her enthusiasm. "I'm visiting your area for the first time and wondered what activities you could recommend for my family." I gestured to my wife and daughters still looking at brochures on the other side of the room. "Our daughters are six and eight years old."

The cheerleader sprang into action saying, "Ready? Okay! I know exactly what your kids would love. If you drive just a few blocks down South Court Street, you'll see a parking area along the bank of the Tennessee River. We have an old railroad trestle, converted to a pedestrian bridge, that extends out over the river to an island in the middle of the water. You can walk out there, free of charge, to view the river. Parking is also free." Then she began quoting a speech that volunteers working at the visitor center were encouraged to memorize. "From this vantage point one can employ the mind's eye to imagine the great steam vessels of the nineteenth century, known to locals as showboats, plying the waters of the majestic Tennessee River. These luxury liners of the Old South featured beautifully appointed state rooms, gambling saloons, and music parlors where banjo players and fiddlers entertained guests for square dances and cocktail parties."

The cheerleader paused to take a drink from her water bottle, and I interjected before she could continue painting her romantic picture of moonlight and magnolias. "Did I understand you correctly? This is just something to imagine while standing on the bridge. There is no actual steamboat my children can ride."

"You are correct. But don't worry, they will still really enjoy it, because on the island, right off the end of the railroad trestle, there's a big dead tree. It's traditional to take your underwear off and throw them up into the branches."

Before I could stop myself I blurted out, "I'm not going to do that! And I'm not going to encourage my children to do that either. Good grief, I already have trouble keeping clothes on my six-year-old."

The cheerleader stopped bouncing, but only for a moment. She quickly recovered from my rebuke and turned to the volunteer standing next to her, the man in the sunglasses and t-shirt. "Jake, you have kids. What would you recommend?"

Jake barely moved. He just slid a paper map across the counter towards me as he said, "Rattlesnake Saloon."

I asked with more than a little fear and trepidation, "What's that?"

"Can't tell you. It would spoil the surprise."

For a moment, I thought about trying my luck with the third volunteer, the lady dressed in purple, but remembered bad luck comes in threes and decided to leave well enough alone. Turning back to my family I said, "Saddle up kids, your maw and me are going to take you to the Rattlesnake Saloon!"

We hopped into the car and headed out. My wife, consulting the trail Jake had blazed on the paper map, pointed out the railroad trestle spanning the Tennessee River as we drove down South Court Street on our way out of town. My children were very excited to spy the underwear tree on the island. Eventually, we left the city and the river behind as we drove down a two-lane highway past fields and farms and into deep woods.

Just about the time I thought we were lost, my wife said, "There it is … I think."

Tacked to a telephone pole was a sign with "saloon" hand-printed above an arrow pointing down a gravel road that disappeared among the trees. I turned the car onto the road, and we traveled about a hundred yards before coming to a small clearing. Standing in the middle of this area was a little structure not unlike what we used to call a school bus shack. Just a little homemade lean-to to protect you from the weather while you waited for your ride. After parking the car, the four us walked over to the school bus shack and stood inside. My wife and girls were looking at me expectantly.

I finally said, "Let's wait here ten minutes. If nothing happens, we'll go back to the visitor center."

Nine minutes into our pre-determined ten-minute wait, a John Deere tractor pulling a hay wagon came rolling up from a wide path on the far side of the clearing. The man driving stopped in front of the school bus shack and asked, "Y'all want to ride?"

I answered, "I don't know. Can you take us to Rattlesnake Saloon?"

"That's where I'm going," he assured me.

My wife looked at me and said, "Is this safe?"

I answered honestly, "We're about to find out." I lifted my two girls into the hay and helped my wife climb aboard before I clambered up and over the wheel to join my family atop the wagon.

The tractor driver said, "Next stop, Rattlesnake Saloon."

My wife asked, "Do you make other stops?"

"Naw, not really. I guess I should say 'Rattlesnake Saloon is your final destination.'"

My wife gave me a look not unlike one Ma Ingles might have shot at Pa just before they headed west into dangerous Indian territory.

The tractor made a lurching U-turn and traveled back down the wide path from whence it came, this time with us on board. In about a hundred yards we came to a field of standing corn. Along the side stood several round corn cribs with peaked roofs made of corrugated tin. At the end of the row there was a building that looked like a little country store. The tractor pulled up in front of it and the driver said, "Just go in there. She'll be glad to help you."

We all climbed off the hay wagon and opened the screen door to discover who "she" might be. We found ourselves in a little gift shop with shelves stocked with jams, jellies, baskets, corncob pipes, coonskin caps, rock candy, and lots of other pioneer paraphernalia. A lady behind the counter dressed in blue jeans and a gingham top reminiscent of the television show *Hee Haw* asked, "Do y'all need a room?"

"No, we already have lodging in town at the Hampton Inn," I explained.

My wife immediately stepped forward to take over this conversation. "These are our daughters, Libby and

Bethany," she said, gesturing to the girls who were looking at some wooden yo-yos and whirligigs displayed on a small table. "Libby is eight and Bethany is six. We are here ... maybe ... to see Rattlesnake Saloon."

The lady in the gingham blouse smiled knowingly. "Oh, of course you are. I thought y'all wanted to spend the night. We rent out corn cribs as family accommodations."

My wife shot me another Ma Ingles look and I took the conversation back. "Can you tell us what the saloon is exactly?"

"Oh, no. I wouldn't want to spoil the surprise. Just follow the path outside this building. Go down and around the ridge. You can't miss it."

As we started down the path that led even further into the woods, I heard my wife mutter, "Rattlesnake Saloon, and our girls are wearing flip-flops."

✧✧✧

It turned out Rattlesnake Saloon wasn't at all dangerous. Not in the least. There weren't even any rattlesnakes. No live ones, that is. The path led around the ridge, which opened into a giant cliff that provided a natural shelter for an outdoor restaurant of sorts. Since it was only ten in the morning, the place was completely deserted. We made our way between dozens of empty tables and chairs to the very back of the cliff, where a set of saloon doors led to the entrance of some sort of cave. We were greeted by four girls in gingham tops and Daisy Dukes leaning over a Monopoly board spread out on the bar.

One of them looked up long enough to say, "Hey, we ain't open for service until noon, but if the kids want to see the snake, he's over there."

She waved a hand toward a large, plexiglass box sitting atop the opposite end of the bar before turning her attention back to the game. We walked over to examine a diamond-back rattlesnake which, through the magic of taxidermy, had been frozen in a coiled strike position for at least forty-seven years. Other than a complimentary Coke for each of us, that was pretty much it. My wife did let the girls use her cellphone to take a selfie with the snake, but the experience wasn't exactly a Kodak moment for my family.

Skipping a second hayride, we took a short path through the woods to get back to our car. It wasn't even noon, so most of the day was still before us. Returning to the visitor center, I left my family in the car while I popped inside to inquire about alternatives to Rattlesnake Saloon and the Underwear Tree. The three volunteers I met earlier were still ensconced behind the information desk. Since I had already received recommendations from Jake and the cheerleader, I had high hopes when I approached the purple lady, altering my previously negative thinking to the third time would be the charm. I began by saying, "I like your fashion ensemble. Is purple your signature color?"

She replied with enthusiasm equal to that of the cheerleader. "Purple is the official color of our local school, The University of North Alabama, Home of the Purple Lions!"

"Would there be something like a science center or a museum at the university my children might enjoy?"

"A zoo habitat counts as both a science center and a museum, and we have one right on the front campus. It houses our two mascots, a male lion named Leo and a female named Una. Your kids will love them. The lion enclosure is just six blocks from this location. Walk straight up South Court Street and continue onto North Court Street. Just listen for the roaring."

I thanked the purple lady and hurried back out to the car to tell the family, "We've been to a saloon, now we're going on a safari!"

Leaving the car parked at the visitor center, we started walking up the street. By the time we got to the third block, you really could hear a lion roaring in the distance.

My wife asked, "Where are we going?"

I told her what the lady at the visitor center had told me. "The home of the purple lions!"

My two children suddenly stopped walking and asked in unison, "They're purple?"

"I'm not sure," I replied, "but it's most likely one would see a purple lion after visiting Rattlesnake Saloon."

My wife smirked at my little joke, and the kids' excitement began to build when we heard another roar as we approached the gated entrance to the campus. It was easy to find the lion habitat. Once we walked through the front gates, we just followed the purple pawprints painted on the pavement.

The lion habitat was like a miniature African plain with high grass in one area, a shallow wading pool in another, and several shade trees. There was also a big, flat rock high up on a bank where the king of beasts could stand surveying the entire campus of the University of North Alabama. The enclosure was surrounded by a double row of iron bars. The outer bars were obviously to keep spectators at a safe distance. The much taller inner bars actually contained the big cats. Between the two sets of bars ran a sidewalk, allowing the animals' caretaker to safely walk all around the enclosure.

We immediately saw the female stretched out atop the big, flat rock taking a nap in the sun. The male was flopped on the ground right up against the inner bars. A woman sat in a lawn chair on the sidewalk just outside the bars reading a paperback novel.

I asked, "Are you the lion keeper?"

She put the book down and stepped closer towards us. "Yes, I sure am. I raised both of these cats by hand. They slept in a cardboard box right beside the refrigerator in my kitchen when they were just babies. I fed them formula from a bottle."

My eight-year-old asked, "Why did they sleep beside the refrigerator?"

"Because the humming of the motor sounded like their momma's purr, and the warm air blowing out from under the fridge kept 'em from getting cold at night."

Then my six-year-old wanted to know their names.

"This big boy sleeping next to me is Leo. And that one up on the rock is his sister. Her name's Una."

"Oh, I just assumed they were a breeding pair, but they're actually siblings," I said.

"Yeah, I've heard all the jokes about this being Alabama and how folks marry their kin, but they've been fixed, so we don't have nothing like that going on."

My wife wanted to know if we indeed had heard them roaring as we came up the street.

The keeper assured her, "Oh, yeah honey. That was Leo here. He roars several times before he lays down to take his nap. He probably won't roar anymore for a while, but would you like to see him do a trick?" My girls were very excited. "All right then," said the lady. "Get your cell-phone ready so you can take a picture."

She stepped toward the sleeping lion and reached between the bars to slap him on the nose. Leo opened one eye and yawned, his mouth gaping wide open as saliva dripped off his fangs. Then he chomped his mouth shut, closed his eye, and went right back to sleep.

My girls were expecting something more like a circus act. Libby asked, "Is that his only trick?"

"Yeah, that's pretty much it. He's done for the day. Lions sleep fifteen to twenty hours a day."

Both of my girls turned to me as Bethany asked, "Can we go?"

I thanked the lion lady for the information and the trick before we started back to our car.

By now it was high noon, with the sun beating down on us from overhead. It was admittedly hot, the kids were tired and hungry, and we were all just a little ... underwhelmed.

The girls started complaining. "I'm bored." "I'm hungry." "I want to go back to the hotel!" "I want to go swimming!"

My wife tried to reason with me. They were little kids, it was lunchtime, everybody was cranky; maybe some food and a swim would be the best thing. I made the argument we could go swimming anytime; we should take advantage of the day. Suddenly, my older daughter, Libby, stopped walking and put her hands on her hips. Libby is not extremely vocal; that's my younger child, Bethany, who like me, rarely has an unexpressed thought. So when Libby has something to say it's worth hearing.

She looked up at me and said, "Daddy, we want to go swimming because we need to wash the weird off."

I couldn't argue with that, but I was still frustrated. My wife suggested we return to the hotel where she would feed the kids and take them swimming, leaving me free to explore on my own. After dropping the family off at the hotel, I inexplicably returned to the visitor center. Some might say I was being a glutton for punishment, but I like to think of it as persistence that paid off, because I was finally awarded an interview with none other than the director of tourism. She told me the three volunteers I met earlier were on their lunch break and she was working the information desk herself. Her name was Helen. When I relayed the woeful tale of our family's fruitless efforts to find a fun and educational activity, she simply said, "I'm so sorry." With genuine sincerity and southern speech, not to mention she was wearing a lady's seersucker suit, I was confident that at long last I was speaking with someone who understood exactly the type of thing I was looking for. "I would highly recommend driving to the neighboring hamlet of Tuscumbia to visit Ivy Green."

"May I ask what I will find there?"

"Certainly, Ivy Green is the childhood home of a world-famous author, activist, and lecturer."

"My goodness," I exclaimed. "Who lived there?"

"Well," said the director of tourism, "She happens to be my namesake—Helen Keller."

I couldn't believe my good fortune. I had read Helen Keller's autobiography years earlier and was thrilled to learn I was now standing just a few miles from her home. Following a map provided by the director of tourism, I found Ivy Green without any trouble.

When I walked up to the front porch of the historic house, a tour guide met me on the steps. "Hello, my name is Mary. Helen called to inform us you were coming. She would like for me to give you a personal tour of her namesake's home with her compliments."

As Mary opened the front door of the historic property and I stepped inside, I immediately felt right at home. I had visited many historic homes, but this was the only one in which I already knew exactly where everything was located. Helen Keller had so thoroughly described her childhood home that every detail came rushing back to my memory.

When I said as much to the tour guide, she nodded and said, "Your experience is not unique. People who have read Helen's book often say that. Since you know your way around, feel free to walk about the house and I will be available to answer questions."

Just inside the front door and to the right was Captain and Mrs. Keller's bedroom. I remembered Helen's father was a Civil War veteran and her mother was originally from Memphis. After seeing their room, I went directly upstairs to see Helen's bedroom, which was separated by a little breezeway from the bedroom of her teacher, Anne Sullivan. Helen locked her teacher inside her bedroom once and hid the key, forcing Captain Keller to fetch a ladder and help Miss Sullivan climb out the window. Beneath the stairs was a broom closet where, on another occasion, Helen did the same thing to her own mother. A gardener found Helen sitting on the front porch steps with a key in her hand, laughing to herself, and realized what had happened when he heard Mrs. Keller pounding on the door and yelling for help.

It was shenanigans like these that caused Anne Sullivan to say, "Oh, she is smart, but she needs discipline. I know the education of this blind and deaf child will be the distinguishing event of my life, if I have the brains and perseverance to accomplish it."

In the back of the house, on the left side of the hallway, was the entrance to the dining room where Helen learned to fold her napkin. It was one of the first lessons in civilized, disciplined behavior Anne Sullivan taught her. Plates were broken, forks were bent, and food was thrown, but in the end, Helen folded her napkin. After seeing the dining room, I exited through the back door to see a water pump standing in the middle of a small, brick courtyard. No, not *a* water pump, *the* water pump where the light began to dawn for Helen as Anne Sullivan poured the cool liquid over her hands and she blurted out her first word: "water." That moment is vividly described in Helen Keller's autobiography. It is also dramatically presented in the award-winning stage play *The Miracle Worker,* which has been translated into film several times starring the likes of Anne Bancroft, Patty Duke, Melissa Gilbert, and Hallie Kate Eisenberg. Seeing the very spot where one of the most dramatic moments in the history of American education took place was thrilling.

Mary, who had been following me from place to place asked, "Do you have any questions?"

"Only one. Can I go get my daughters and bring them back to see this?"

"Of course. I would love to meet your girls."

I drove back to the hotel and found my wife sitting under the shade of an umbrella watching the kids play in the swimming pool. I quickly explained what I had discovered, and she agreed the girls should not miss such a wonderful opportunity. We hauled them out of the water and quickly dressed them. On the way back over to Ivy Green, I told them a very condensed version of Helen Keller's story. Then I asked my tour guide to lead them through the house.

Mary was wonderful with my kids. She took great delight in pointing out things that would interest young girls. They enjoyed running around inside of Helen's "hedge of protection," which was a circle of box hedges Captain Keller had planted to make a sort of outdoor playpen for Helen when she was young. They also loved hearing about Helen's tree-climbing adventure. Mary told us that story at the conclusion of our tour as we were walking back to our car. Near the parking area stood a huge magnolia tree. No one knows whether it was the exact tree, but she said it was a good spot to tell the story.

It seems that after Helen learned to communicate through sign language, Anne Sullivan realized she had missed out on so many things sighted and hearing children took for granted, like learning how to climb a tree. So, on a summer's day they had climbed a tree together. While sitting in the branches, Miss Sullivan had signed into Helen's hand, "It is a beautiful day. You stay here while

I go back to the house and make some sandwiches so we can have a picnic lunch up in this tree."

Helen readily agreed and her teacher climbed down and walked away. While Miss Sullivan was gone, a freak storm blew in and poor little Helen Keller, unable to hear the thunder or see the lightning, rode out the storm while clinging to the bow of the tree. We all had a good laugh when our tour guide Mary told us that Helen Keller said, "It was a thrilling experience, riding out a thunderstorm up in a tree. I highly recommend it and think everybody ought to do it at least once."

My children talked and talked about Helen Keller all the way home from Alabama. They started climbing trees in our backyard. I was grateful for the memory we made but thought that was the end of it. The very next year I was invited to return to the same festival. Knowing how memorable the tour of Helen Keller's childhood home had been for my own kids, I thought about my friend Dean Walters, who taught deaf children at a local elementary school in my hometown. I called him to ask if there was some way we could give a long-distance tour to his students using the camera on my smartphone. Dean said, "Certainly, you can just walk around with your phone and I'll project what you're seeing on the digital board in my classroom. As you talk about what we're seeing, I can translate it into sign language for my students." Then he added, "Tim, you probably don't realize what a big deal this would be to my kids. We watch *The Miracle Worker* every year and Helen Keller is like a patron saint to them."

When I called Debbie Chaffin, the director of the Shoals Storytelling Festival, with a special request, she assumed I wanted to bring my family back when I returned. I explained all I wanted was a couple hours to give the tour to Dean's students and she very generously said, "Oh, no. We can do better than that. We will just make that part of your duties. Instead of giving a concert in the theater that day, you'll conduct a virtual tour of Helen Keller's childhood home." Then Debbie, always looking for an angle to promote her festival, said, "This is going to be big. I'm going to call all the local TV stations and send a press release to national media outlets. We're going to be on *Good Morning America*! I just know it!"

We ended up with quite a production. The logistics were a bit complicated, but the tour went even better than expected. Entering a room, I told a brief story as Debbie panned the scene with my cellphone camera while Dean translated my words. Then the kids signed questions, Dean translated, and Mary provided the answers before we moved on to the next room. We were not picked up by any national broadcasts, but a local TV station covered the story. Ironically, I was giving a tour of the Helen Keller home with my cheap smartphone while a professional TV crew followed us around with their fancy five-thousand-dollar camera and high-end sound equipment.

Finally, we came to the water pump where Helen had spoken her first word. While Mary was chatting to the kids in Charleston about the details of the story, I noticed an older couple, grandparent age, standing off to the side curiously watching. I stepped off-camera and explained to them what we were doing, then said, "I have an idea. Would you be willing to step in and greet the children on camera and let them teach you how to sign the word for water in American Sign Language at the very spot where their hero learned how to speak the word 'water?'"

The couple readily agreed. We stepped over to the water pump so I could introduce them and tell everyone else my idea. When Dean translated that these hearing people wanted to learn how to speak sign language, the students in his classroom got so excited they rushed the camera. For several seconds all we could see were fingers flying in front of the lens and we could hear Dean laughing. After a bit of commotion, he got the kids to step back and teach us how to make the sign for water by holding up three fingers to make a W then touching the sign to our lips as if to drink. Standing at the water pump in Helen Keller's backyard, we were learning to speak with our hands and hear with our eyes. And through the small screen on my smartphone, we entered the deaf world where the joy on the children's faces was evident.

Mary turned to me and said, "I never met Helen Keller, but I am confident in saying she would have loved this!"

✵✵✵

I have told stories at more than fifty festivals and for nearly a quarter million schoolchildren, and I've never had a more rewarding experience. After our tour was concluded and the kids from Charleston logged off, I thanked everyone who had helped to make the event possible. Then I called my wife and kids to tell them all about it. As I drove home to South Carolina, I realized that not only bad luck, but good luck too, often comes in threes. I had visited Helen Keller's home alone, with my own children, and—through the wonders of technology—with my friend Dean and his students. Just as I had assumed before, I thought that was the end of it. But less than a year later, I found myself standing in my office looking at a wall calendar filled with storytelling gigs, all of them marked "CANCELLED." With tears streaming down my cheeks, I turned to face my family saying, "I cannot tell stories on Zoom."

But my daughter Libby, the girl of few words who was now nearly ten years old said, "Daddy, you already have. You and Helen Keller."

ROMUEL AND SAMUEL

My daughter asked to go fishing for her eleventh birthday. I love my daughter, but do not share her enthusiasm for sitting by the water's edge waiting for nothing to happen. There are a couple popular fishing spots near our home, and since it was her birthday, I promised we could try our luck at both. We planned to begin at the Jessen Boat Landing, behind the Aldi grocery store on Dorchester Road. If we caught nothing there, we could drive a few miles to Ashley River Park, where there is a stocked fishing lake. Bright and early—that's another reason I don't like fishing—we found ourselves sitting on the wooden dock at the Jessen Boat Landing. I didn't even bother to take a fishing pole for myself. I planned to simply bait hooks, cast off, pull snags, and untangle the line for my daughter. I had no sooner got her pole all rigged up and cast a baited hook into the water when I had the feeling someone was watching us. Handing the pole to my daughter, I turned around to discover two gentlemen standing no more than three feet from me. How they got that close without us even hearing their approach I could not guess.

If I'm fifty-four years old, these fellows were every bit ten years my senior. Obviously identical twins, they were dressed in perfectly matching outfits—bright white tennis shoes, blue jeans, and red hoodies—and rocking in unison, back and forth, back and forth, in that distinctive way common to many people on the autism spectrum.

Before I could say a word, they stopped rocking and struck a pose, sort of like Fred Astaire with jazz hands. One of them said, "We sing and dance."

To which I replied, "Of course you do. I would know fellow showmen anywhere." Taking a business card out of my pocket and handing it over I added, "I tell stories."

The twin who had spoken snatched the card and stared at it intently as his brother looked over his shoulder before asking, "Can we keep this forever?"

"Certainly," I assured him. "That's why I have them printed. I give them out all the time."

The second man took the card from his brother and tucked it into his pocket saying, "We should get some of these."

Then the first one announced, "We are going to do a show for you."

Without further introduction, they immediately began to croon "I Want It That Way" by the Backstreet Boys, with perfectly synchronized smooth moves to accompany the song. When they finished, one or the other, I don't remember which, asked, "Did you like that?"

It was obvious they had rehearsed this routine many times, and I praised their perfectly executed choreography, but mentioned the Backstreet Boys were not my favorite group.

The twin who had first spoken to me immediately inquired, "When did you go to high school?"

When I said I graduated in 1988, they instantly began moon-walking across the fishing dock in a manner that would give Michael Jackson a run for his money as they performed his whole "Billie Jean" routine step for step. After this five-minute number had ended, I applauded their performance.

The first gentleman, who seemed to be the spokesman for this dynamic duo, asked "Did you like that one better?"

Before answering, I glanced at my daughter, who would tell you I seem to attract characters like these two gentlemen. She just grinned, shook her head, and went back to tending her fishing line. I interpreted this as permission to encourage these two brothers in their show business endeavors. Turning back to the twins I said, "Well, Michael Jackson was certainly popular during my high school days, but I never really got into pop music. I've always loved classical."

They obviously interpreted "classical" in a completely different way than I meant and started gyrating Elvis Pelvis-style and belting out "You Ain't Nothing But a Hound Dog." When they finished this third number, I praised their knowledge of classic rock and roll. They asked me if I had any other requests, but I thought it best not to mention Bach's "Toccata and Fugue in D minor."

Doing my best to change the subject I said, "Gentlemen, I would like to introduce you to my daughter, but I don't even know your names." I was quickly informed they were identical twins, Romuel and Samuel. Romuel, the brother who seemed to always take the lead, told me that he was the oldest by one minute.

"It's nice to meet you," I replied. "I'm Tim, and this is my daughter Bethany."

Just about that time, Bethany said, "Daddy, can you check my line? I'm not getting any bites."

I reeled in the line to confirm there was still a worm on the hook. As I cast it back out into the river, I said, "Romuel, my daughter is trying to catch a fish, but nothing seems to be biting. Do you know a song that might help?"

He immediately started slapping his forehead with the palm of his hand and saying to himself, "Fish, fish, fish." Finally, he announced, "I got it." He grabbed my right hand and lifted it skyward, closed his eyes, and began to sing in his best Celine Dion, "Near, far, wherever you are …"

Immediately, Samuel picked up the tune. Humming a harmonic accompaniment, he stepped to my other side to grab my left hand and raise it into the air. The three of us stood there on the fishing dock swaying back and forth. As the two showmen continued the theme song from *Titanic*, my daughter just bowed her head. I hoped Romuel and Samuel would interpret her gesture as reverence, but I knew it was actually mortification. When the last phrase had been sung, Romuel opened his eyes.

As we lowered our hands, he took mine and kissed it, saying, "Brother, if that don't bring the fish, nothing will!"

My daughter continued to keep her head bowed. I intuitively knew she needed some space, so I invited my new friends to step to the other end of the dock with me. After we had established a little distance, allowing Bethany to fish in peace, I said, "You guys are so generous to share all these songs, plus you even sang an extemporaneous number to call the fish. I should return the favor. Do you know the song 'I'm Going Crazy?'"

They both shook their heads and gestured for me to sing it. Without further prompting, I shared the silly song from my childhood that I learned at summer camp.

"Once there was a mama dog,
And all she'd eat was cans,
So when those little puppies came,
They came in Ford sedans.

Once there was a mama cat,
And all she'd eat was yarn,
So when those little kittens came,
They came with sweaters on.

Mary had a little lamb,
The doctor was surprised.

When Old MacDonald had a farm,
The doctor nearly died."

By the time I belted out the final chorus, Romuel and Samuel were humming along and clapping their hands.

"I'm going crazy!
Don't you want to come along?
I'm going crazy,
Just singing this song."

My performance was a big hit. Not only did I receive enthusiastic applause, Romuel gave me a glowing review by slapping me on the back and saying, "You so funny! I wish you were little so I could put you in my pocket. Then, whenever I felt down, I could just take you out, wind you up, and you would sing your little song for me."

My daughter, still fishing at the other end of the dock, was looking toward us with an expression that could only be described as bemused embarrassment, when she said, "Daddy, I still haven't caught a fish."

I was still glowing from the rave review I had just received from my audience of two as I replied, "Honey, you may not be catching anything, but my net is full!"

She quickly reminded me, "Yeah, but you promised."

The twins stopped laughing. Romuel earnestly inquired, "What did you promise?"

I began to explain. "Well, today is my daughter's eleventh birthday ..."

That was as far as I got. The two men leapt back to the other end of the fishing dock shouting, "Is it your birthday, Baby Girl?" My daughter nodded. "Do you like cartoons?" Romuel asked.

Fortunately, I had taught my daughter to lie when it's the polite thing to do. She doesn't really care about cartoons, but she smiled and nodded. Of course, that was all the affirmation these two characters needed as they launched into a Popeye and Olive Oyl bit, dancing up and down the fishing dock, cracking jokes, and performing pratfalls for a full eight minutes. My daughter just sat there with her fishing line dangling from the end of her pole, watching these two clowns give their best slapstick performance in celebration of her birthday.

When they finished the routine, she thanked them, then repeated to me, "I still haven't caught a fish."

I turned to explain to Romuel and Samuel I had promised to change locations if the fish weren't biting, realizing my explanation would sound like a made-up excuse. I felt bad, but it really was the truth. "Gentlemen," I said, "I am truly sorry we can't stay, but I promised Bethany if the fish weren't biting here, we would try a different spot. I'm afraid we have to go."

The guys looked a little crestfallen but seemed to accept what I had said. I was helping Bethany collect her things when Romuel said, "We understand you have to go, but let us sing you just one more song."

I looked at Bethany and she nodded. "Okay, just one more, then we have to go."

The guys each put a hand on my shoulder and started to sing. I was so taken aback by the lyrics that I stopped them. "Wait, wait, wait. Can you start over? I want to make sure I understand all the words."

Romuel replied, "You got a phone?"

I pulled my phone out of my back pocket and gave it to him. He handed it to Samuel, who immediately opened YouTube and cued up Jordan Hill's "Remember Me This Way" from the children's animated film, *Casper.* "Here. You can follow the words while we sing."

The melancholy lyrics remind the listener that people are often separated by physical distance, circumstances, time, and eventually death; but true friends are always together in spirit. As the song concluded, both brothers reached up and placed a hand on either side of my face, touching my temples with their fingertips as they sang for me their parting wish "that life would be kind to such a gentle mind."

I just stood there stunned. Eventually, I realized my daughter was holding my hand. My voice cracking, I said, "I'm so sorry guys, but we really have to go."

Bethany started to pull me away and the guys followed us, with Romuel saying, "We're going to walk you to your car." I apologized again as we put the fishing rod, tackle box, and bait bucket into the trunk. "We understand," the older twin replied, "but let us pray for you."

I tearfully nodded.

The twins threw their arms over our shoulders as Romuel lifted his eyes skyward and began to pray aloud. "Lord, Baby Girl needs to catch a fish for her birthday."

As it turned out, Bethany didn't get a single bite at the second spot either. And we haven't seen Romuel and Samuel since. But we are not without hope, because of how Romuel ended his prayer.

"They gotta go, but let us be reunited in Hollywood where we can do a show together!"

ABOUT THE AUTHOR

Tim Lowry decided he was going to be a showman when he was six years old and has fulfilled this self-proclaimed destiny by becoming a professional storyteller.

After graduating from college, Tim moved to Charleston, South Carolina and drove a horse-drawn carriage before becoming an English teacher. While his storytelling talents served him well as a tour guide, it made his teaching methods "unorthodox and disruptive" according to the administration. He left the classroom for the stage in 2000 and has now performed for hundreds of thousands of delighted audience members, including, ironically, over 250,000 schoolchildren.

Tim joined the National Storytelling Circuit in 2012 and has appeared at over fifty festivals. He has also provided workshops for large organizations, including Dollywood Dream More Resort and United Way. His most told story is not one of his own, but rather Charles Dickens' *A Christmas Carol*, which he has performed more times than Dickens himself.

Now he's sharing his stories in print as well as in person. His first book, *Haunted by Dickens*, weaves his humorous personal tales into Charles Dickens' most famous story. It also discusses the many themes found throughout the book.

Southern Fried Circus is his second book.